Developing an Explosive Offense

Charlie Stubbs

©2006 Coaches Choice. All rights reserved. Printed in the United States.

No part of this book may be reproduced, stored in a retrieval system, or transmitted, in any form or by any means, electronic, mechanical, photocopying, recording, or otherwise, without the prior permission of Coaches Choice. Throughout this book, the masculine shall be deemed to include the feminine and vice versa.

ISBN: 1-58518-945-6
Library of Congress Control Number: 2005932451
Cover design: Jeanne Hamilton
Book layout: Jeanne Hamilton
Diagrams: Deborah Oldenburg
Front and back cover photos: University of Tulsa Sports Information Department

Coaches Choice
P.O. Box 1828
Monterey, CA 93942
www.coacheschoice.com

Dedication

This book is dedicated to my loving parents, Joe and Sue, who have always been shining examples for me to follow. To my wife, Sandy—who continues to exhibit love and support as we share the disappointments and triumphs of a coaching career. To my children—Troy, Jay, Kimberly, and Kyle. You have been great—always providing me with special experiences and unconditional love.

Acknowledgments

As is usually the case, the completion of this book was made possible through the help, guidance, and teamwork of a number of people.

I wish to thank assistant coaches Robert Anae, Dabo Swinney, and Mark Weber, who contributed position group and drill information. I especially want to thank Coach LaVell Edwards for writing the foreword.

My gratitude is also expressed to the staff at Coaches Choice, particularly Dr. Jim Peterson for giving me the opportunity to give something back to the profession that has been great to me.

Finally, I would like to acknowledge those in the coaching profession, too numerous to list, for their friendship, commitment to the game, and contributions to the philosophy and material outlined in this book.

Light up the scoreboard!

Contents

Dedication ...3
Acknowledgments ...4
Foreword ...6
Introduction ...8
Chapter 1: Establishing an Offensive Philosophy ...9
Chapter 2: Coaching the Quarterback ...20
Chapter 3: Formations and Pre-Snap Movement ...41
Chapter 4: The Passing Game ...57
Chapter 5: Protect the Quarterback ...77
Chapter 6: Innovative Practice and Game Planning ...99
Chapter 7: Mini-Topics ...114
Chapter 8: 25 Explosive Offensive Plays ...140
Conclusion ...166
About the Author ...167

Foreword

Early in my coaching career, a very famous college football coach supposedly made this statement: "Whenever you throw a pass, three things can happen and two of them are bad." That was the general attitude of most coaches for decades.

When I became head coach at BYU in 1972, I inherited a program that, in 47 years of football, had averaged a little over three victories a year, and had won one conference championship and no bowl games. Because of the weak program and the difficulty in recruiting the nation's top athletes due to the restriction of a private university, I decided that we were going to have to do something different. We had to come up with a program that would create interest with the fans and would help us level the playing field in terms of being competitive. The one year that BYU had success, 1965, was when Virgil Carter was the quarterback and we threw the ball. After winning the conference championship, the pass went back into mothballs and wasn't much of a factor in the ensuing years, a fact reflected in the record. I decided that we would resurrect the pass and hopefully break the pattern, not only at BYU but also throughout the country.

As a single-wing coach and a defensive coordinator, I was not the person to put the offense into action. I set the philosophy and then gathered people around me who could develop the package into a viable offense. Each year we tweaked it a little bit, refining as we learned. Fortunately, I had some creative minds around me and they were able to take what I had visualized and make it work. For the next 15 years, most defenses were confounded and we lit up the scoreboard. Passing didn't do it alone, of course. It took a sound running game with running backs who could also catch the ball, a solid defense, and effective special teams, but it was definitely the forward pass that got the program out of the mire.

Even now that the defenses have adjusted, good execution still makes the forward pass an amazing tool. There really isn't any phase of offensive football that is as great of an equalizer of talent than the forward pass, with the use of formations, motion, and the wide variety of passes, such as the three-step (quick pass), the traditional five-to-seven step dropback, the sprint out, the misdirection or naked pass, and myriad play-action passes available. Over the years, various coaches at many universities and in the pro ranks have refined the package and created new and different uses of the forward pass.

Charlie Stubbs is one of these coaches. Charlie worked for us at BYU, the first stop in his quest to master the passing game. He came with a solid understanding of the game of football and he absorbed everything possible while he was here. He has gained knowledge and experience with each coaching opportunity and has been an intense student of the continuing evolution of the offense. He has an offensive mind and personality and has learned, through study and experience, how to get the most out of the talent available. And he has learned how to do it with humor and keep the element of fun in the game for the players, coaches, and fans.

Developing an Explosive Offense is a must for any football coach who wants to improve his philosophy of offensive football. It has concepts that can be utilized from youth football through the pros. It's a great reference book or a manual around which to build an entire offensive package. It's a wonderful addition to the football publications library.

—Coach LaVell Edwards

Introduction

Through the 1970s and early 80s, successful football programs were ground-oriented. Even as the wishbone and veer went out of favor, the I formation remained. In the mid-80s, however, defenses underwent a great change with the rise of the press (in-your-face), an attacking variation of the 46 Defense, which had carried the Chicago Bears to a Super Bowl title in '86. Extreme versions of the press placed at least eight defenders close to the line of scrimmage to take away the run. Any team with two good cornerbacks capable of covering man-to-man could shut down an opponent's ground game without fear of getting beat deep. Offenses had few answers.

Developing an Explosive Offense is one! It discusses utilizing multiple formations (lots of spread alignments) and motions. In response, defenses must decide whether to cover each receiver man-to-man, drop into a zone (bailing out of the press), or stick with the press and count on hitting the quarterback before he can deliver the ball to an uncovered receiver. In any of these options, the defense is reacting to the offense.

As you read this book, I believe you will be exposed to numerous ideas, concepts, and principles for developing an explosive offense. Furthermore, I want this book to be an invaluable reference text for players and coaches at all competitive levels and even the fan or football enthusiast.

Football is a game that evolves, with each new coach adding their own wrinkles even as they are indebted to the great coaches before them. I am a product of many coaches, learning from them all—while at the same time trying to add my own innovations and adjustments to give the players a better chance for success. Men like LaVell Edwards, Dave Kragthorpe, and Mike Holmgren have had a major impact on my development as an offensive coach and I can trace many of my theories back to them.

The book includes numerous diagrams and charts that will help clarify and illuminate specific concepts.

Hopefully, this book will be extremely useful to you, regardless of your basic system and philosophy. If *Developing an Explosive Offense* provides readers with a tool that enhances their ability to reach the next level of success, then the efforts to write this book will have been worthwhile.

1

Establishing an Offensive Philosophy

Coaching a successful offense unit is very complex and requires a good amount of organization. In establishing an offensive philosophy, it is important to follow a few basic principles to ensure success. Many different offensive designs are available and numerous ways exist to successfully move the football, so you, as coach, should give considerable thought to what is important. Limit the offense to what can successfully be practiced, and, in turn, what the team can execute well. Many coaches have a tendency to overcoach and use too many plays, rather than undercoach and have too few plays in the offense. Decide what approach to use and then develop an offensive philosophy around that particular approach. By staying with the same approach year after year, you enable your players to become highly skilled in the fundamentals of the offensive scheme by the time they reach the varsity level or are in position to be a starter. Coaches who change offenses from year to year will never have the continuity required to develop a high level of execution.

A team also needs a fully developed offensive system that provides it with the flexibility to access whatever phase of the offense it needs, whenever it needs it. A fully functional approach features a balanced offense that accounts for all reasonable situations that can occur during the game. It provides a system to address each situation as it develops.

Other factors to consider when establishing an offensive philosophy include:
- Athletic ability of players
- Style of defense—football is a team game
- Knowledge/coaching ability of staff
- Opponents/competition—points needed to win
- Climate/field conditions
- Past experiences—learning from other coaches/mentors

The remainder of this chapter offers a detailed outline of how to establish an offensive philosophy.

General Team Goals for Winning

- Be tougher than the opponent
- Be smarter than the opponent
- Be in better condition than the opponent

Winning Strategies

Field position and opportunism—Give the opponent the long field and then be opportunistic by taking advantage of every good field position that is provided.

Ball control and points—Control the ball (keep the defense off the field as much as possible) and be a point-producing offense.

Mistake-free football wins—To win a game, a team must first keep from losing it. With the proper emphasis in practice, a team will not self-destruct during the game. Do not beat yourself by turning the ball over or stop a drive by committing a needless penalty.

Offensive Strategies

Offensive flow—Create a rhythm or flow to the offense that will often produce the deciding momentum. This rhythm should be felt in practice and internalized so that it can be generated again in a game.

Beat opponents to the punch—Gain the advantage by repeatedly beating the opponent to the punch with quickness and explosiveness. This will eventually wear down the opponent, which will often be a deciding factor.

Second effort—Believe in the ability and the desire of a blocker to sustain just a little longer, and of a receiver to extend just a little farther. Often, this will be a deciding factor in the game of inches.

Communication—Much of the detail and precision of the offense can only be "fine-tuned" by communication—from coaches to players, players to coaches, and coaches to coaches.

Play the hand you're dealt—The maturity, poise, awareness, and flexibility to adjust to changing situations will often be a deciding factor between winning and losing.

Will to prepare—Concentrating in meetings, doing extra film study, and practicing with rhythm, as well as effort and detail, is a part of the price that must be paid to win.

Let it flow, let it go—Proper preparation will allow players to play uninhibited without fear of making a mistake. True ability will only show itself in this type of environment.

Design—The purpose of design is to put players in positions to utilize their talents. Flexibility, communication, and consistent concepts are keys in allowing players to win.

Tell each player: "Be a football player"—Gray areas are sorted out by players. Instinctive players can make things work in these situations.

Mix-Down Strategies

- The objective is to be successful enough on first downs to remain in a mix-down, or unpredictable, situation for the defense.
- A two-to-one run-pass ratio on mix downs is most productive. Substituting a control pass for a run in this situation can also be productive.
- Utilize formations and personnel groups that allow both run and pass to be effective.

Running Plays

- Basic zone combination blocking and run-to-daylight plays are a good scheme.
- Combination blocks are utilized when the defensive alignment allows for more aggressive line takeoff.
- Other blocking patterns are game-planned as change-ups.
- Game-plan your runs from the outside in—what is the best way to get outside on this particular opponent? Utilize formations and motion schemes to reduce force and make the defense play more base-type defenses.

Downfield Combination Passes

Basic dropback protection incorporates a big-man rule—offensive linemen are assigned to defensive linemen and backs are assigned to backers. This rule should eliminate a size mismatch for the backs or a quickness mismatch for the linemen. Also, by assigning the backs to backers, they can be incorporated into the pass pattern should their backers drop into coverage. Slide protection is used to help when needed versus a four-man rush.

Basic route design is to give an all-purpose route that will allow the offense to attack the defense whether it is in zone, man, or combo coverage. Versus zone, two potential receivers are placed on one zone defender with enough vertical or horizontal separation between them to make it impossible for the defender to cover both. Against man, adjustments are built in to give each receiver the best chance to beat his defender one on one. Versus combo, the responsibility is for the single-covered receiver to beat his defender and for the quarterback to get him the ball.

When game-planning, first decide what will work against an opponent. Next, decide what can be executed with the most effectiveness. Finally, decide what can be worked on enough to have game-ready. Generally, go into a game with about 10 to 12 mix-down, downfield pass combinations. A complete understanding of concept, precision, and adjustment is a key ingredient in this phase.

Control Passes

- When a control pass can be used as a running play, it should be completed (i.e., 100% completions).
- A control pass is designed with a high-percentage downfield pattern and dump-type outlet. If the downfield throw is threatened at all, the pass should go to the outlet.
- A few patterns are particularly good for this purpose. For this reason, the use of different formations is very important to this phase of the attack. The looks can be changed up without changing up the patterns.

Home Runs

- Three basic reasons exist as to why to go for the home run. First, a reasonable chance exists for hitting it—otherwise it would not be in the game plan. Second, it keeps defenders from squatting on the receivers. Third, an unusual amount of pass interference penalties are called on bombs.
- The basic design is to get the best single-coverage match-up on a takeoff route and let it fly. To the other side, build an all-purpose route that should be good when not getting the proper coverage for the bomb.

Long-Yardage Strategies

- Third down conversion rate is a critical factor. Every conversion over what the opponent makes represents about 40 yards of field position.
- Defensive strategies generally fall into three basic categories:
  - ✓ Third-and-three to -six—Defenses like to play tight combination- or man-free-type coverage and mix in some dog. They cannot afford to sit back in a soft man-to-man or zone coverage and let a quarterback pick undercoverage apart for first down yardage.
  - ✓ Third-and-seven to -12—Defenses mix their coverage more in this situation. Generally, they will play combination and man-free robber-type coverage and mix in a small amount of zone. In this situation, defensive strategy is to combine rush and coverage to stop the offense.
  - ✓ Third-and-twelve-plus—This is a zone coverage situation. The defensive strategy is to give up the underneath throw and make the tackle before the receiver can run for the first down.
  - ✓ In addition to these basic strategies, defenses will employ a pressure package to some degree. It is important to identify what this package is and how it is used. Is it used on third-and-12 to force the sight adjust, or is it used as a momentum changer?
- The offense should feature spread formations in long-yardage situations.
  - ✓ These formations spread the defense and allow the offense to attack the width and depth of the field in a variety of ways.
  - ✓ The quarterback's gun alignment makes it easier to protect his launch point, gives him more vision, and allows him more time to deal with pressure.
- The four- or five-receiver out protection scheme incorporates hot reads. Vision and communication are critical.
- Use a quarterback-under-the-center formation as a change-up. The added run threat and the quarterback being able to receive the snap and throw more quickly from these formations make them suitable for third-and-three to -six or second-and-long situations.
- Motion schemes are particularly important in long-yardage situations when press-type coverage can disrupt timing and downfield stretch. Motion schemes are designed to allow a quicker release in a preferred direction.
- Placement of personnel is a big key in the long-yardage attack. Place a slashing receiver with one who has a lot of burst and allow them to run the routes for which they are most suited.
- Three basic approaches exist in pattern design that correspond with the defensive strategies:

- ✓ Third-and-three to -six—Stay to one side with lateral bursting routes and hitch/curl-type routes. Also, drag routes are effective.
- ✓ Third-and-seven to -12—Use pattern combinations designed to defeat specific coverages. It is the responsibility of the receiver that is singled to separate from his defender and for the quarterback to get him the ball. At times, build a zone pattern to the opposite side and go to it versus a zone coverage. With very few exceptions, routes are not adjusted to distance. If the route does not take the receiver to first-down depth, then he should attempt to pick up the needed yardage with the run after the catch.
- ✓ Third-and-12-plus—Use pattern combinations designed for zone. Often, the defense will force the offense to throw a n underneath route. If the receiver is unable to pick up the first down with the run after the catch, at least field position is gained.
- Take shots in long-yardage situations for the same reasons as in mix downs, plus one. There will be times that the chances of hitting a shot are as good as picking up a third-and-very long.
- The third-and-long run package serves three purposes. First, a reasonable chance of success exists—otherwise, it would not be in the game plan. Second, it gives the defense more to think about than rushing the passer and playing pass defense. Third, it can be a percentage play when in field goal range or when backed up.
- This package can also be used in second-and-long situations.

Goal Line and Short-Yardage Strategies

- On the goal line, the offense must score a touchdown. At the very least, the offense should be effective on 90% of its goal line plays.
- The offense should be 85% effective in short-yardage situations.
- The offense cannot afford to move out of these high efficiency situations by committing a needless penalty.
- The opponent will be playing a desperate, gambling style of defense. Be alert for very quick, low, penetrating inside charges on slants.
- Cut line splits to one foot to prevent inside penetration, and to allow your offensive linemen to utilize combination blocks.
- Most of the time, a close formation will help control an aggressive perimeter force or blitz.
- Use a simple snap count so that the offense can concentrate on beating the opponent to the punch. Vary the snap count in short yardage in an attempt to draw the defense offside. However, only use this strategy when game planning indicates a strong advantage.

- At times, in short yardage, and more often on the goal line, the defense will commit additional people to stopping the run. Be alert for an inside dog by an outside backer and a perimeter blitz from a secondary defender. On the goal line, this additional pressure will be in very short-yardage situations or often on first down. If the offense can be stopped on the first down, it creates a more predictable situation for the defense to handle.
- First down is the best time to throw the ball on the goal line. With the tendency to commit additional people to stopping the run in this situation, coverage will be reduced.
- The defense is more willing to gamble on offensive tendencies. The offense should be aware of its own tendencies so that a defensive scheme designed to stop a play can be anticipated.
- Be alert to the opponent's tendencies or substitutions that would indicate a goal line defense in a short-yardage situation.
- Utilize formations and motion schemes to reduce the force, or fill, or to manipulate a slant. Also, because of the communication problem that it causes the defense, use motion if it does not affect the play.
- The offense should block low enough to match the opponent's charge to keep them covered and get push at the same time. Use combination blocks where feasible to provide more push.
- Be secure with ballhandling.
- The ballcarrier should start quick, read quick, and lay out to the hole. He should know the situations and design of the play and know when to go over the top for the score or first down. In short yardage, he should run for the sticks before looking for extra yards.

Red Zone (+20) Strategies

- The offense should score with either a touchdown or a field goal.
- Do not turn the ball over, take a sack, or commit a penalty that will take the offense out of field goal range.
- Most defenses will become more desperate the closer the offense gets to the goal line. Know what yard line, what down and distance, and what scoring combination will trigger the opponent into their plus-20 philosophies.
- It is important to identify the opponent's plus-20 philosophy. Some teams will use a "send them all" concept. Others will utilize moderate pressure and tight coverage. Finally, an increasing number of teams simply maintain their in-the-field philosophy. These teams depend upon containment and offensive self-destruction.
- Because of the short field, many teams choose not to give post help. Instead, they use combination coverage in an attempt to take away offensive strength or tendency.

- An increasing number of teams will use zone coverage in this area of the field because of the variety of formations, motion schemes, and personnel groupings that offenses can utilize. Also, the fact that most teams have a capable back that can be involved in downfield routes also suggests coverage.
- Self-scouting is an important item in the plus 20, as a defensive team becomes more desperate. They will be more willing to gamble on offensive tendencies.
- As the field shrinks, it becomes more difficult to move the ball. For this reason, the offense should try to score quickly by increasing the ratio of pass attempts in this area of the field.
- The pass plays in this area of the field incorporate certain principles. First, utilize formations in an attempt to create a mismatch or single coverage for a receiver to run a downfield route designed to score. Second, provide the quarterback with a simple outlet if the defense is not in the right coverage. Third, because a pressure defense is likely, utilize quicker drags, crossing (rubs), and rhythm patterns. Fourth, use sound protection schemes. Fifth, stress blitz control (hot principles).
- Have set mix-down and long-yardage run and pass plays.

Coming Out Strategies

- The first objective is to move the ball out to the five yard line where a normal spread punt can be used. Also, try to make at least one first down before having to punt.
- Most defensive teams play an aggressive, containing defense. Be alert for an inside charge by the forcing unit in an attempt to shut off the straight-ahead play. Their objective is to hold the offense to three yards or less per play without risking giving up a 98-yard home run.
- Some teams will gamble by committing more people to stopping the run. Be particularly alert to this style of defense when backed up inside the one or two yard line. These schemes will often incorporate linebacker dogs and perimeter blitzes.
- Cut line splits to two feet to prevent inside penetration and to allow linemen to utilize combination blocks.
- Use a simple snap count so that the offense can concentrate on beating the opponent to the punch (also, utilize a hard count).
- Utilize formations and motion schemes to reduce the force, or fill, or to manipulate a slant.
- Keep the opponent covered and get push at the same time. Use combination blocks where feasible to provide more push.
- Be secure with ballhandling.
- The ballcarrier must start quick, read quick, and lay out quick for the hole.
- Have a set three-run play sequence designed to get out of the backed up area.

- Have a mix-down pass play and a nickel pass play for the appropriate situation.
- Have a set nickel run for the appropriate situation.
- Have a play set for when backed up inside the one yard line.

Run-Out-the-Clock Strategies

- The objective is to run out the clock. At times, this will require the offense to pick up a first down. If unable to pick up the first down, at least use up as much time as possible.
- Keep the clock running.
  - ✓ Ballcarriers must stay in bounds.
  - ✓ Do not call a time-out.
  - ✓ Use near the full 25 seconds between each play.
  - ✓ Do not ask for a measurement after first or second down.
  - ✓ If less than 25 seconds are left, let the clock run out without leaving the huddle.
  - ✓ Do not stop the clock by committing a needless penalty, which is one reason to use a simple snap count.
- The opponent will be playing a very desperate style of defense. Be alert for a very quick, low, penetrating inside charge or slant.
- Because offenses are reluctant to throw the ball in this situation, the defense can commit additional people to stopping the run. Be alert for an inside dog by an outside backer and a perimeter blitz from a secondary defender.
- Most of the time the offense will use a close formation to help control an aggressive perimeter force or blitz.
- Cut line splits to two feet to help prevent inside penetration.
- Be secure with ballhandling. A ballcarrier should overprotect the ball and not run with such abandon that he gives the defense a shot at the ball.
- The attack will consist of short yardage–type run plays. The offense will also carry one or two very high-percentage pass plays. If a pass is called, it must be completed.

Two-Minute Offense

- The two-minute offense should be employed when your team is behind with less than two minutes to play. Work with quickness and poise, knowing that techniques are available to stop the clock and that only one out of four plays need to be successful to keep the drive alive.
- The two-minute offense can also be used near the end of the half. However, be conservative in this situation. The decision to use the "hurry-up attack" will be based

on the time remaining, the score, and the risk factor—the offense cannot afford to turn the ball over, nor can it stop the clock with incomplete passes, giving the opponent time to score.
- The defense will be playing with one of two styles:
  - ✓ If the opponent feels that they can stop the offense with the clock or long field, they will often utilize maximum zone coverage that protects the sideline.
  - ✓ If the opponent feels that their defense must stop the offense, they will use rush plus coverage. This means that they will employ a four-man rush and utilize combination coverage along with zone coverage, or they may decide to be aggressive with a combination of dog and blitz. Have a plan to deal with both situations.
- Use basic offensive concepts.
  - ✓ Utilize set procedures at the line of scrimmage.
  - ✓ Utilize one snap count.
  - ✓ Utilize one basic formation.
  - ✓ Use a time-out:
    - Before a fourth down play.
    - At five seconds when you are in field goal range and need the field goal to win.
    - When the clock is running with less than one minute left and two or more time-outs remain.
    - After a long gain (20+ yards) and two or more time-outs remain. Officials will stop the clock to reset the down markers.
    - After a sack—because valuable seconds will be lost before the ball is reset.
  - ✓ Have set pairs of huddle plays (three sets of two).
  - ✓ Have the last three plays of the game set.
  - ✓ Have last-chance plays for the following situations:
    - Plus five
    - Plus 10
    - Plus 20
    - Outside plus 20
- Have a thorough understanding of what stops the clock.
  - ✓ A called time-out.
  - ✓ An incomplete pass—never throw the ball away to stop the clock on fourth down.
  - ✓ A ballcarrier goes out of bounds.
  - ✓ A penalty—unless an offensive penalty is considered intentional. In some situations, the referee may start the clock after penalty yardage has been marked off.

✓ When the officials have to move the chains, or an unusual delay occurs in spotting the ball, in which case the clock starts on the referee's signal.

Audible Philosophy

- Trouble audibles are used to get out of a potentially bad play. Use a trouble audible anytime that a pre-snap look indicates trouble for a play.
- Advantage audibles are used to take advantage of specific defensive weaknesses. They can be divided into two categories:
    ✓ Potential big play
    ✓ Better play than the one called in the huddle

Advantage audibles are based a lot on "feel." The quarterback should really "feel" that the play would be successful for him to audible to it. A common sense principle exists regarding when to use an advantage audible. For example:

✓ When trying to control the ball late in the half or game, stay with a high-percentage play—do not audible to a potential big play. A solid play such as a run will consume more time and has more value than "a chance" at hitting on a big play on third down.

✓ When nearing field goal range, a high-percentage play to advance the ball may be more important than "a chance" at hitting on a big play.

2

Coaching the Quarterback

The one person most responsible for an effective offensive attack is the quarterback. He is an integral and important part of the offense and his ability alone will often make the difference between a good attack and an average one. The quarterback should have outstanding athletic ability, be superbly coordinated, mentally alert, and physically strong.

Leadership is a basic quality necessary for a good quarterback. Very seldom will you find a successful quarterback who is not a leader—someone whom the other players respect and will respond to in critical situations. The quarterback does not have to be loud or vocal, but he should possess an attitude that exudes confidence and self-assurance. Many leaders are vocal and lead by encouragement, while others are not vocal but express themselves through physical actions. Regardless of the method, the quarterback should be the leader of the offense.

The quarterback should also be intelligent. He should know the assignments of all 11 players on the offense and have a good knowledge of any defense that opponents might use.

The quarterback initiates every offensive play. Therefore, his athletic skills, mental capacity, and leadership skills must be evident. He should be willing to constantly work on the development of his physical fundamentals and skills.

In reality, no single "blueprint" exists for the ideal skills and traits a quarterback should possess, or how much of each characteristic a quarterback should have. However, effective quarterbacks are courageous, competitive, spontaneous, adaptable, and mentally and physically tough.

Great quarterbacks will:
- Always give a great *effort*.
- Be coachable—*listen*.
- Stay *positive* in all situations.

Qualifications Desired in Selecting a Quarterback

Athletic Ability to Make Big Plays

- Passing ability—passes on time and is accurate
- Running ability—"escapability," which is the ability to avoid the pass rush

Leadership and Confidence

- Is consistent in everything required of him (e.g., drills, meetings, academics)
- Is a coach/motivator on the field and leads by example
- Is confident in his abilities

Poise

- Thinks clearly and maintains composure
- Doesn't allow negative criticism to affect his performance (i.e., is "thick skinned")

Note: A quarterback receives too much credit when his team wins, but will also receive too much blame when his team loses.

Intelligence

- Has the ability to learn the complete offense
- Understands defensive strengths and weaknesses
- Makes correct decisions both mentally and physically
- Is a student of the game

Quick Hands and Feet

- Has the ability to execute all quarterback movements—is a complete player

- Is smooth and efficient—no wasted movement

The Ten Commandments of the Quarterback

- I will always lead my team with the best of my natural ability.
- I will never fumble an exchange from center.
- I will always put the team first.
- I will carry out my fakes on every play.
- I will always be sharp, calm, and confident.
- I will never make a mental mistake.
- I will never lose sight of the team's objectives.
- I will improve every day as a player and person.
- I will be an example for others to follow.
- I will be persistent.

Quarterback Fundamentals

Quarterback fundamentals are the key to success. A coach or player should never place scheme before fundamentals. The most common mistake in the installation of an offense is to put in plays before proper technique has been taught. The following outline provides the details of quarterback fundamentals and techniques.

General Techniques

Stance

Feet—Comfortably spread, about as wide as the shoulders, and either parallel (toe to toe) or staggered. The quarterback should be as close to the center as possible. Most important—he should be consistent and make necessary adjustments on the snap.

Knees—Bent comfortably, but not strained.

Hips—The quarterback should drop to a comfortable position and remain as tall as the center will permit. He must see the defense.

Arms and Shoulders—Bent slightly forward, shoulders even with the center's hips.

Head and Eyes—Straight ahead or moving from side to side, reading the defense.

Balance—The quarterback must remain balanced until the last possible instant before the snap, then transfer the weight to the stable foot (push-off) to prevent a false step.

Poise—The quarterback should remain relaxed and reflect a confident attitude. He should never hurry the play.

Hand Position (Right-Handed Quarterback)

Upper Hand—Right hand up, palm parallel to the ground. The quarterback should position the wrist deep and flat, arm bent, and elbow close to body. He should extend and spread the fingers strong but not tense. The hand should press firmly against the center's crotch to create a target and follow-through for the snap. This is the receiving hand.

Lower Hand—The left hand should be aligned thumb-to-thumb and wrist-to-wrist with the right, pointing downward toward the feet. The fingers should be extended and spread similarly to those of the right hand. This is the support hand, used to trap the ball.

Snap

Laces—The quarterback should give the laces to the center and adjust his fingers after the snap.

Exchange—The ball should be received by the upper (right) hand, centered in the groove of the palm. The lower hand traps the ball in the support position. The throwing hand should receive the laces for quick throws.

Follow-through—Both hands should follow the center as he charges forward. Proper hand pressure encourages this.

Head and Eyes

Pre-snap—The quarterback should examine the pre-snap look while approaching the line of scrimmage and continue reading the progression throughout the cadence, looking for possible audibles.

Look—Upon receiving the snap, the quarterback should turn the head quickly to locate where the ball will be placed, keeping the eyes fixed.

Pocket—After the follow-through, he should bring the ball into the body at the belt area, with the elbows close to the sides. He can then adjust for the hand-off.

Step—Patterns vary with the play called. Generally, the quarterback must step to deliver the ball as deep and/or quickly as possible. Teach the quarterback to allow the eyes to determine the length of the step.

Fake—The type of fake varies with the play. Options include following the hand-off to check for a fumble, looking to the second option, and eying the defense to hold the secondary.

Pass—The quarterback's eyes should be downfield reading at all times—during cadence, snap, drop, and through the release.

Signal Calling

Huddle

Teach your quarterback to take complete charge of the huddle and assume the role of "captain," even if he isn't truly the team's captain. A quarterback must be able to get everyone's attention and follow the following progression.
- Formation
- Play
- Snap count
- "Ready… break." Always encourage a sharp, loud break, as this breeds confidence. It all begins here.

Line of Scrimmage

A good quarterback is calm, patient, and most importantly, confident. The commands are signals, not simply numbers being called. Have your quarterback follow this progression:
- Check the defense on the way to the line of scrimmage and allow the offense to reach the pre-shift position.
- Place the hands under the center and use the command "ready" to give the signal to shift.
- Pause to allow initial movement.
- Call (fake) audibles in a series.
- Command "set."
- Pause and check alignment.
- Use non-rhythmic cadence using the words, "hut…hut, hut," etc.

Running Game

Position of the Ball

Post Snap—The quarterback should use "pocket" technique, bringing the ball into the body at the belt area with the elbows close to the side. This allows him to secure the ball.

Adjustment—He should adjust his hands on the ball according to what is to be done next.

Before Hand-Off—The quarterback should keep his body between the ball and defensive man he's trying to deceive. He should carry the ball low and comfortably prior to the hand-off.

Pivots, Spins, and Turns

Head and Eyes—Instruct your quarterback to turn his head and eyes in the direction of the spin, locating the ballcarrier and junction point. He must be under control to avoid any contact with the lead blocking back.

Shoulders and Hips—These techniques require a twist from the hips and shoulders in a natural motion, following the head and eyes. Again, stress balance and control.

Footwork—The initial "push-off" begins when the ball is received, never before. A transfer of weight should precede the push-off, shifting from a balanced position to the stable away foot. The lead foot steps in the direction of the play in a swinging motion and should be kept close to the ground. The following procedure should be smooth and sound:
- Head and eyes turn in the direction of the play.
- Shoulders and hips follow under control.
- Push off with the away foot with a proper transfer of weight.
- The lead foot steps in the direction of the play.
- Follow through with the push-off foot for balance; move in controlled alignment.

Hand-Off

Responsibility—The quarterback is 100% responsible for the success or failure of the hand-off. He must adjust to the receiving back and get him the football. Tell your quarterback to "see" the ball into the ballcarrier's pocket.

Holding the Ball—The quarterback should keep both hands on the ball as long as possible. When approaching the placement point, he should move the ball from the pocket to the ballcarrier while gradually releasing the hand nearest that point. The give hand should be slightly under and to the rear of the ball. Remind your quarterback: "start with two; finish with one."

Look—Instruct the quarterback to first watch the spot where the ball is placed. He should then look the ball directly into the belt buckle and make any necessary adjustments.

Footwork—The quarterback should try to make the exchange with the same foot as the give hand. Although this is not tremendously important, it allows for greater reach and balance.

Placing the Ball—The quarterback must place or press the ball firmly into the ballcarrier's pocket (remembering to adjust to him), thereby allowing the give hand to ride the ball. The ball should be motionless and not placed too high, as this is a source of fumbles. He should avoid slamming the ball into the ballcarrier.

Faking

After the hand-off, the quarterback should return his hands to the pocket for additional fakes or to set up to pass.

Three main types of fakes exist:
- Show the ball with two hands, ride the fake, and pull out.
- Hold the ball in the pocket area with the support hand while placing the empty give hand at the placement point, allowing the back to fold over it.
- Post-Play Faking—Several options include a "boot" look, additional handoffs, and setting up to pass.

Purposes for completing the entire fake include:
- Deception of the defense
- Protection from getting hit from behind
- Opportunity to read the secondary (pass fake)
- Becoming the safety man in the case of a fumble

Passing Game

Position of the Ball

Technique—After following through the snap, teach the quarterback to bring the ball into the pocket position and continue to high-cradle it at armpit level, using both hands and adjusting the laces to the fingers. The arm should be cocked and ready to throw at any time. He should never carry the ball in one hand.

Throwing Mechanics (right-handed quarterback)

Footwork—Upon reaching the set up position, the quarterback should anchor his final step and close his feet in a gathering motion to prevent overstriding. The quarterback should be perpendicular to the line of scrimmage until a decision is made to throw the ball. At this point, he should step toward the target with the left foot and never cross the imaginary line drawn from the right foot to the receiver, and never step too far left, either. The quarterback should not overstride; instead, he should stay on top of the left foot through the passing motion. The follow-through should take the rear foot past the front foot and toward the target.

Read—The quarterback must locate the defensive man on the drop, and make a decision on where to throw. He should find the receiver or the seam and take advantage of "looking off" secondary defenders who are reading him. This can be done during the drop, after the read, or whenever the opportunity arises. The main point is to keep the eyes on the target through the throw.

Arms and Shoulders—The quarterback's arms should be kept close to the body until the pass action begins. At this point, a cocking action takes place in which the left elbow passes the left hip immediately prior to the first forward movement. As the ball is thrown, the right elbow should be above the right shoulder for proper throwing action. Teach the quarterback to follow through completely.

Hand Position—This technique is largely a matter of personal preference and success. Basically, the ball should leave the index finger last and the palm should face the target at all times. The follow-through should emulate an inverted position.

Throwing Short—Short- to medium-range passes should be thrown at normal speed using the techniques outlined thus far. An important point is to avoid overstriding; the quarterback must throw while over the front foot.

Throwing Long—Only in this passing situation should it becomes necessary for the quarterback to overstride slightly and throw more off the back foot. The trajectory of the pass is such that this step is necessary. He should throw the pass knowing the speed of the receiver as well as the position of the defensive secondary. Generally, the quarterback should release the ball with the idea of letting the receiver run under, adjust, and catch the ball in stride.

Screens and Swing Passes—These passes should be thrown in a way that is similar to the short pass technique, without extra loft but at a speed that may be less than normal. The quarterback must adjust to the location of the receiver (find a passing lane).

Dropback

Steps—Short routes call for a three-step drop, medium routes a five-step drop, and long routes a seven-step drop.

Types, Techniques—Three basic types are employed:

- Crossover—This technique is conventionally used in all three drops and involves dropping the tail to begin movement and momentum, utilizing a lead step with the right foot parallel to the line of scrimmage, and performing a crossover to the set-up point. In the last steps before the anchor, the quarterback should shift the weight forward to slow down and prepare to gather the feet.
- Backpedal—The quarterback should begin by dropping the tail as in the crossover, dropping the right foot first to facilitate the same three- five- and seven-step drops. This method allows for easier reading, but is not as quick as the crossover.
- Combo—This technique is used in five- and seven-step drops and employs the crossover method from the line of scrimmage. When two steps from the set-up position, the quarterback pivots on the right foot, turns his body to face the defense, and continues the final two steps in a backpedal.

Sprint Out

Ball Position—The quarterback must get the ball to the high cradle position immediately after the snap, and prepare to throw at any point. He should carry the ball here until the decision is made to run or throw.

Footwork—Teach the quarterback to open with the onside foot and run to get outside. He should try to get six-to-seven yards deep as quickly as possible and square the shoulders to the line of scrimmage or main receiver. He should also continue a controlled sprint an throw off of the right foot.

Philosophy—The sprint out pass is designed to take advantage of a quarterback who runs well and can exploit defenses when containment is easily broken. A simple rule would be to run when he can get at least five yards or when no receivers are open. The quarterback should always try to avoid letting a defender get a solid hit.

Throwback

From Sprint Right—The quarterback should follow the same procedure for a sprint out, but anchor approximately behind the tackle, which should require about five steps, and prepare to throw. His eyes should read from sprint out side to the throwback at the anchor position.

From Sprint Left—Two methods can be used upon reaching the anchor position. A reverse pivot is sometimes used, but the preferred method is to step up while facing the line of scrimmage for reading purposes. This is also normally a five-step action using the left foot to plant while dropping the right foot behind. The quarterback should be perpendicular to the line of scrimmage at this point.

Play-Action

Footwork and Faking—These aspects of play-action are dictated by what play fake is called. Obviously, the idea is to sell the run in every way.

Ballhandling—As discussed in the "Faking" section of the running game, the quarterback should hide the ball until the last possible instant before setting to throw.

Reading—Teach the quarterback to follow the fake; this not only convinces the defense of the run, but also allows the quarterback to continue into the reading progression.

Set and Throw—The set position is also determined by the play fake; however, the throwing mechanics are the same.

Bootleg

Technique—Have the quarterback make the play fake and then place the ball on the hip, hidden from the defense. He should sprint with the idea of running, though some plays are specifically designed to throw. He should not rush the fake and should always know what the play is designed to accomplish. Remind your quarterback to always take a pre-snap look at the defense to anticipate edge pressure.

"The Great Quarterbacks Do the Little Things"

Game Day

This is the day the quarterback gets to match his knowledge and ability with that of the opponents. This is also the day that shows which team was the best prepared, displayed the most poise, made the fewest mental mistakes, and had a total commitment to win. Make sure it is your team. Remember, more games are lost than won. It's a shame to get beat, but it's a tragedy to beat yourself.

Study the Opponent

The quarterback should know every possible piece of information concerning the opponent. He should then coordinate this knowledge with the facts about his own team to direct his team to its most productive and efficient performance possible. The quarterback must:
- Know the opponent's general defensive philosophy.
- Understand the thinking behind their different defensive alignments.
- Know their down-and-distance tendencies.
- Have a thorough knowledge of their secondary personnel and alignments.

- Know who have been their "big play" people.
- Know their goal line alignments and adjustments.
- Be aware of any substitution pattern.

Game Day Notes

Provide the following list to your quarterback as a reminder of the scope of his responsibilities and to provide him with some focus on game day.
- Be positive in everything you do.
- Present a confident attitude to the team at all times.
- Allow no talking in the huddle.
- Learn to relax, stay cool, and retain mental poise regardless of the situation.
- Do not argue with an official.
- Always be sure everyone is ready before calling a play.
- Do not use hand gestures while calling plays.
- Speak clearly and slowly in the huddle. Repeat a call if there is any doubt.
- Vary the snap count.
- There is no need to give a pep talk on all play calls, but there may be some situations where this is desirable.
- Always known down and distance, field position, and time.
- Keep track of time outs.
- Have the play call ready before entering the huddle.
- Call the play with confidence. A bad call is better with authority than a good call with hesitation.
- You may not be right every time, but you should never be in doubt.

The quarterback will be asked to give more of his time than any other position on the team. Normally, a team is only as good as its quarterback. Therefore, he should know more and be more polished than any other player. A great deal of his time will be spent in the following areas:

- *Watching Film*—No way exists to watch enough film of the next opponent. It's the only way to know the strengths and weaknesses of various individuals. Watching film of your own team in past games or scrimmages is the best way to observe and correct faults.

- *Studying Defenses*—The quarterback should know as much as possible about the basic defenses. Know their theory, basic alignments, strengths, and weaknesses.

- *Learning Coverages*—He should know what type of coverage goes with what front, what coverage is dictated by a specific alignment, what coverage takes away what route or pattern, and what is given up in each coverage.

- *Learning the Mechanical Skills*—Your quarterback must be adept in the fundamental skills of the position. The snap exchange, steps, pivots, fakes, and ballhandling should be mastered. He should be able to teach these techniques to others.

- *Knowing the Plays*—A quarterback should know the plays inside and out, including the routes and adjustments, the total backfield action, and the basic blocking designs of each play.

- *Checking Off*—He must also know the when, where, why, and how of checking off, in addition to knowing what play to check to.

- *Snap Count*—Work with all of you quarterbacks to develop a constant snap count. It is important that all the quarterbacks sound as much alike as possible so if a quarterback change is made in the middle of a drive, it does not disrupt the tempo of the offensive line.

- *Dedication*—Most of all, quarterbacks must be dedicated. Proficiency cannot be achieved without dedication in the preceding areas.

- *Improvement*—A quarterbacks should worry about one thing—improving. He should strive to become the best he can possibly be and not worry about others. A quarterback should not worry about being a starter or backup, or what his up-to-date statistics are. Instead, he should worry about improving each and every day. Remind players, "You either become better or you become worse. You can never stay the same, for you will only let others pass you by."

Passing Drills

Each drill is explained with the assumption of a right-handed passer. A southpaw should automatically reverse the words "left" and "right" whenever they are used.

Throwing from One Knee Drill

The purpose of this drill is to improve the grip and to increase the wrist snap. When throwing from one knee, it is not possible to get the whole body into the throw. Therefore, emphasize the wrist snap portion of the throwing motion.

Have the quarterback kneel on one knee, with the knee down on the side of the passing arm. The ball should be placed on the ground about a foot in front of the knee that is down. Using the passing hand, he should grip the ball and lift it from the ground. Once the ball has cleared the ground, the non-passing hand should also be placed on the ball, so that the two hands together lift it up to a point just above the outside of the right ear in passing position. The quarterback makes the throw from there by drawing the ball back as the shoulder is cocked. Remind the quarterback to be very careful to avoid the tendency of "winding up," or dipping the ball way down below the level of the shoulder just prior to throwing.

The quarterback should always try to throw with a straight overhand motion, emphasizing the snap of the wrist just as the ball is leaving the hand. The palm of the passing hand should roll over completely so that the palm is pointing at a 45-degree angle down and to the outside at the completion of the throw. A good passer should develop a considerable amount of wrist snap, so both the coach and the player should be very conscious of this when working on this drill. As with all passing drills, the quarterback should strive to improve accuracy by always throwing at a definite spot. When throwing to another individual 12 yards away, he should aim for a spot such as his nose, or his right shoulder, rather than just throwing the ball in his general direction.

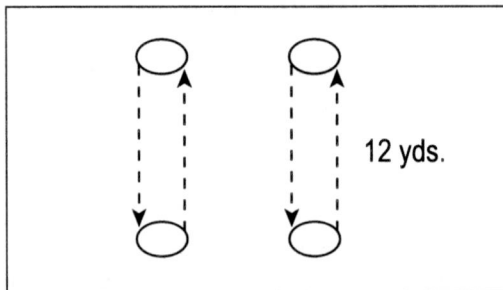

Diagram 2-1. Throwing from one knee drill

Facing Sideways Drill

On most teams, it is just as necessary for a quarterback to be able to throw accurately while rolling out to either side as it is for him to be able to throw from a dropback set position. Although this drill is done from a stationary position, the purpose of the drill is to get the quarterback used to throwing off either foot while sprinting out or rolling out, both to the right and left. The quarterback should throw at least half a dozen times from each of the following four positions:
- At a 90-degree angle to the right of the intended receiver with the right leg forward
- At a 90-degree angle to the right of the intended receiver with the left leg forward
- At a 90-degree angle to the left of the intended receiver with the left leg forward
- At a 90-degree angle to the left of the intended receiver with the right leg forward

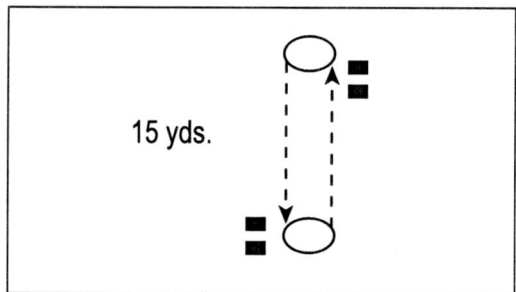

Diagram 2-2. Facing sideways drill

Wrong Leg Forward Drill

This drill is designed to emphasize the importance of getting the entire shoulder into the throw and developing the quick "shoulder cock" just before making the pass. The quarterback stands with the right foot about two feet in advance of the left. He should not move the feet at all while throwing during this particular drill. Since this is somewhat of an awkward position, the quarterback will have the feeling that he will have to push the ball or throw the ball off balance and almost entirely with the arm. Instead, he should use the proper throwing motion by sharply twisting the upper body and cocking the passing shoulder back just prior to making the throw. Have the quarterback throw the ball fairly hard in this drill, as this helps to emphasize the need to quickly draw back the passing shoulder to get any power in the throw. As on most throws, he should use a straight overhand motion, releasing the ball at a point about 18 inches above and outside of the right ear.

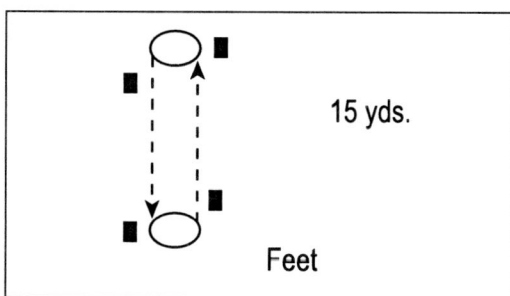

Diagram 2-3. Wrong leg forward drill

Throwing on the Run Drill

This drill emphasizes throwing the ball while moving rather than standing still. When running to the right, the quarterback carries the ball with two hands at chin level and uses the same passing form as on any running play with a "sprint-out" or "roll-out" to the right. When running to the left, as on any running play with a "sprint-out" or "roll-out" to the left, he throws with the same straight overhand delivery.

On any type of dropback, when the quarterback stationary and the receiver is breaking at an angle, it is necessary to have the quarterback throw the ball in front of the receiver. When running in the same direction as the receiver, it is best for him to aim right at the receiver to almost automatically give him the correct amount of lead. Rarely is a roll-out type of pass thrown behind a receiver. When working on this drill, remind the quarterback to consciously aim at the chest of the receiver. This will improve the percentage of completions.

Circle Drill

In this drill, the quarterback will run in circles about 10 yards away from the receiver, and concentrate on leading the receiver, throwing off balance, and turning the shoulders toward the target. This drill should be executed to both the left and right.

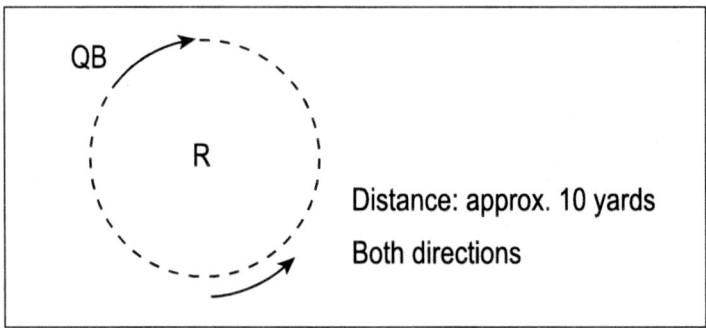

Diagram 2-4. Circle drill

Footwork Drills: Spot Passing

Three-Step Drop

Place three targets (i.e., receivers) on three spots on the field, five, six, and five yards away. Each quarterback should have a ball when coming up to the center.

If no center is available, the quarterbacks can snap to each other. The quarterback should take the snap and a three-step drop. It is critical that he get the ball off on the third step for rhythm. Start by having the quarterback throw to the receiver on the left. After the throw, he should retrieve the ball from the receiver while the next quarterback hustles to the line of scrimmage and begins his sequence. On the second repetition, the throw is to the middle, then the right, and so on.

Emphasis: Rhythm (The quarterback delivering the ball on time)
    Aim point outside—outside armpit
    Aim point inside—middle numbers

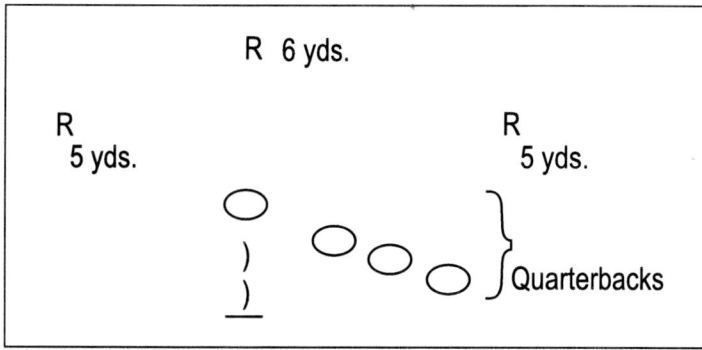

Diagram 2-5. Three-step drop drill

Five-Step Drop

This drill is performed with the same three target areas as the three-step drop drill, but move the targets back to 10 yards, nine yards, and 10 yards, or the quarterback can simply move back five yards.

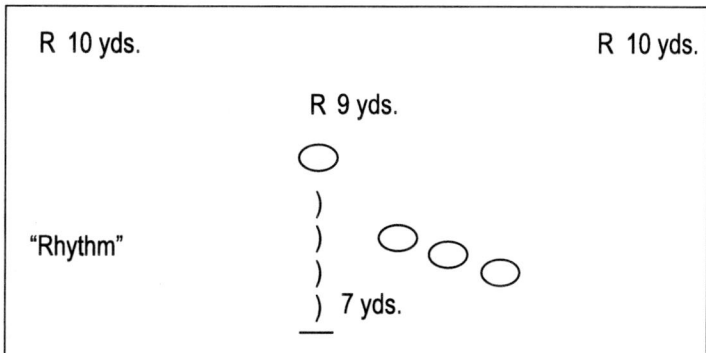

Diagram 2-6. Five-step drop drill set-up

Step #1: Same initially as the three-step drop drill except when throwing to the inside target, when the quarterback should step up and throw. Remind the quarterback to move the back foot first on the step up.

Step #2: Add two linebackers to the drill. The quarterback must keep the feet alive and be ready to read the linebackers. He should throw away or down the middle if they split.

Step #3: Keep the two linebackers in the drill. Still work with the triangle, but the linebackers should not give a read until after the quarterback has begun to slide up and in the pocket. The quarterback waits for a "go" call, and then shuffles forward. The quarterback should move the feet when reaching the drop depth.

Step #4: Incorporate the scramble sequence of the five-step drop pass.

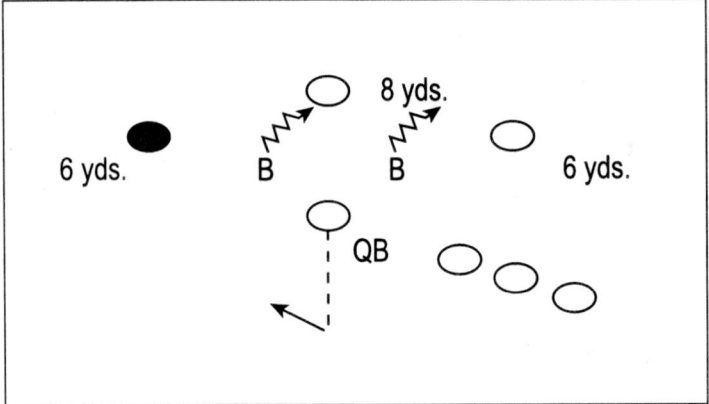

Diagram 2-7. Five-step drop drill—throw away from the linebackers

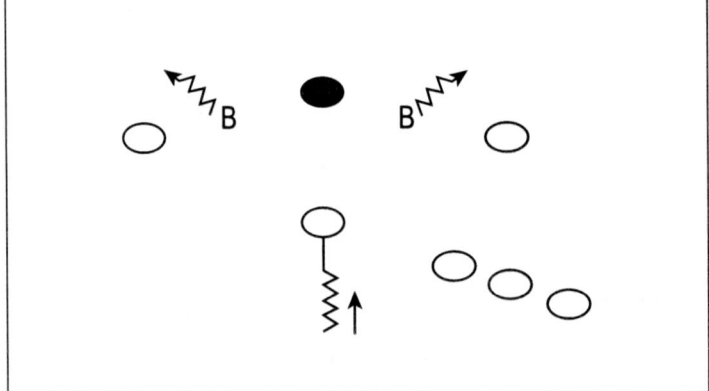

Diagram 2-8. Five-step drop drill—slide up in the pocket

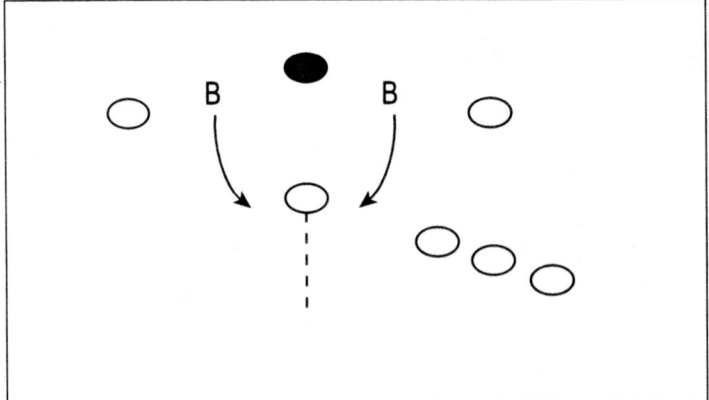

Diagram 2-9. Throw on the fifth step

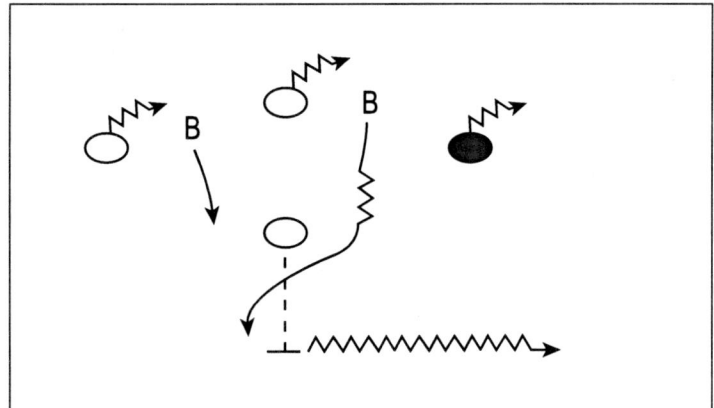

Diagram 2-10. Escape right

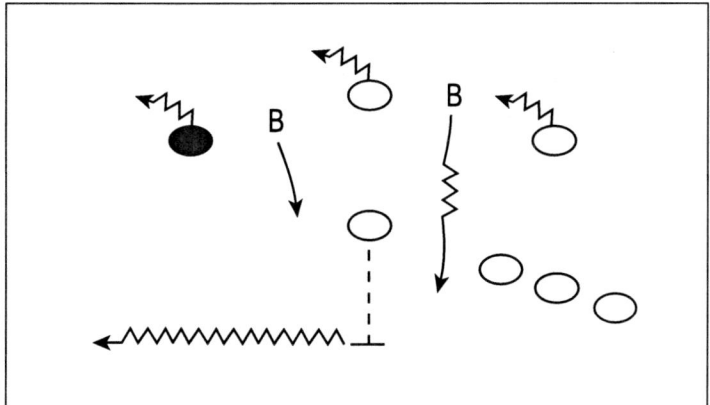

Diagram 2-11. Bail left

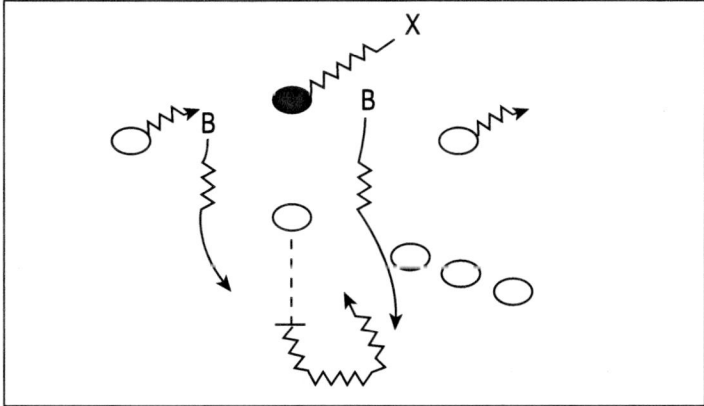

Diagram 2-12. Escape, pull up

Additional Quarterback Drills

Standing Pitch

Two quarterbacks stand five yards apart facing sideways (in the same direction). The quarterbacks practice pitching (with no step), increasing the distance by one yard at a time until they are at least 10 yards apart. Have them perform 10 pitches facing in one direction, and then 10 pitches facing the other.

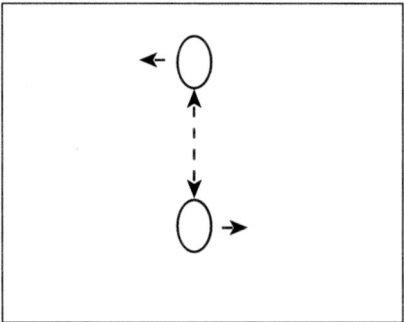

Diagram 2-13. Standing pitch drill

Running Pitch

Two quarterbacks are positioned five yards apart running in the same direction. Emphasize soft pitch while sprinting at full speed.

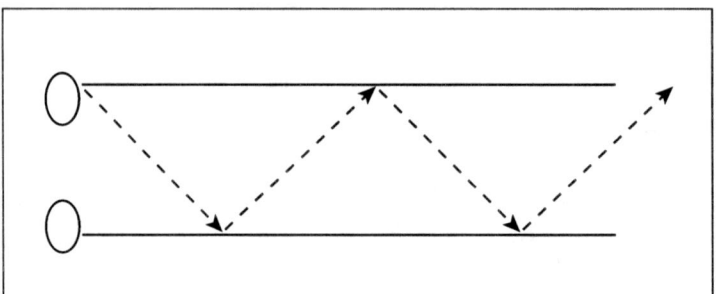

Diagram 2-14. Running pitch

Toss Pitch

The quarterback should use the two-handed scoop pitch from securing the snap with a reverse pivot. Remind the quarterback to always secure the pitch. This drill can also be run with two quarterbacks.

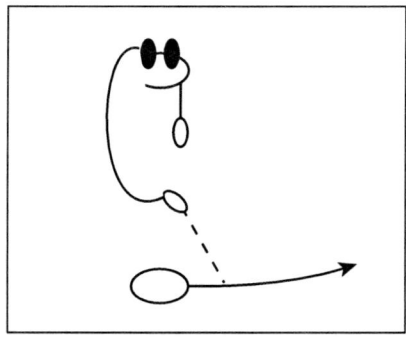

Diagram 2-15. Toss pitch

Sample Practice Progression: Quarterback Drills

Warm-Up Drills (pre-practice)

- Pre-stretch as a group with wood poles
- Center-quarterback exchange
  - ✓ Emphasize exchange (ballhandling fundamentals)
  - ✓ Emphasize footwork and run-game tracks
  - ✓ Emphasize footwork/faking with play-action drops
  - ✓ Emphasize shotgun techniques
  - ✓ Emphasize footwork on drops
- Warm-up throwing drills
  - ✓ Knee throws
  - ✓ Movement throws
  - ✓ Pat-n-go

Footwork Drills

- Spot passing (quarterback sets)
  - ✓ 3-step drop
  - ✓ 5-step drop
    - —Spot passing—rhythm
    - —Target/reaction passing
    - —Shuffle—up pocket (wave drill)
    - —Fifth step hot
    - —Scramble sequence
  - ✓ 7-step drop (can do dame sequence as 5-step)

- Option drill
  - ✓ Emphasize read of the defender
  - ✓ Emphasize pitch to the running back

It is very important to make sure that the quarterbacks have been taught the proper fundamentals needed to play at a high level. *Fundamentals are the key to success.* Many coaches and athletes place schemes before fundamentals. You will not be successful doing this. Each position coach should have a list of drills that will be utilized when coaching his position.

Drill	**Dates**		
Stance			
C/Q Exchange (reg)			
C/Q Exchange (gun)			
Quick Feet			
One-Knee Throws			
Two-Knee Throws			
Sideways Throws			
Circle Throws			
Spot Throws			
Wave Drill			
Flush Drill			
Tracks			
Faking			
3-Step Drop			
5-Step Drop			
7-Step Drop			
Gun Drops			
Dash			
Nakeds			
Sprint Out			
Boots			
Cadence			
Audibles			
Hand Signals			

Diagram 2-16. Quarterback drill progression checklist

3

Formations and Pre-Snap Movement

A thorough and versatile offense includes changing alignments and formations as often as necessary to create confusion among the defenders. Good defensive teams study the tendencies of an offense and then take advantage of this knowledge. It is important for the offensive team to cause hesitation among the defenders whenever possible.

Receivers should vary their alignment (the distance between the wide receiver and the linemen) as much as possible without giving the defenders a clue regarding the play called. Often, the best disguise is for receivers to vary their alignment on a running play, especially if their blocking assignment on the play is not critical. Formation changes can also aid the development of a pass offense. Motion, or pre-snap movement by eligible offensive personnel, should be done with a purpose. The main reason for using motion is to force the defense to change their alignments, coverages, or responsibilities. If an offensive team cannot take advantage of the altered defense, then no valuable reason exists for pre-snap movement.

When developing an offensive attack, it is important to build a system that is flexible. The offense can be added to and expanded by properly utilizing formations, motion, and personnel groupings.

Key Points

- Certain formations and motions can isolate specific match-ups and cause the defense to make adjustments.
- It is important to be able to accurately predict the defensive alignment for a particular formation, which creates a favorable match-up.
- The proper use of personnel groupings can be another key factor to an offense's success. A championship team will get their best 11 players on the field.

Utilizing a Man in Motion

Incorporating a man in motion provides variation to offensive formations. Prior to the snap, an eligible receiver goes into motion to change the strength of the formation. Scouting an opponent's adjustments to motion will often reveal tendencies that will be beneficial in play calling. Using a man in motion offers several benefits to an offense, including:

- It is a fluid way for the offense to change the strength of its formation.
- It forces spontaneous adjustments by the defense.
- It improves the position of the man in motion on his release point on pass routes or blocking leverage on run plays.
- It stretches the defense by attacking different parts of the field with multiple receivers.
- It enables the man in motion to avoid being held up by either the linebackers or defensive backs, particularly versus teams that play tight press/bump and run techniques on the wide receivers.
- It forces the defense to tip its coverage (e.g., zone, man, blitz)
- It isolates individual defenders (e.g., the running back on the strong safety)

Personnel Groups

The proper use of personnel can be a key factor affecting the level of success achieved by a team's offensive system. It is important that a team has its best players in the game to get the job done. If a team's most desirable personnel match-ups can be achieved in a standard personnel grouping (e.g., two running backs, one tight end, and two wide receivers), then that team can gain an advantage on the defense by eliminating one of the factors they use in making their defensive calls (e.g., down/distance and personnel).

It is also important that a team is able to accurately predict the defensive alignment to a particular formation. If the defense responds as predicted, the formation becomes a valid way to take advantage of mismatches. If the defense doesn't respond as predicted, the formation is not a valid way to create the desired mismatch, and in fact may do more harm than good.

Key Points

- Personnel groupings are needed to get an offense's best 11 players on the field to execute a particular play or set of plays.
- The more formations that an offense can align in and execute from without changing personnel groupings will be a major advantage—this will prevent defenses from getting a pre-snap tip.
- The flexibility to break into other formations from the standard alignment will be a significant advantage (e.g., a running back shifting out into a three-wide-receiver alignment).
- Resourceful substitution is an effective method for enabling the offense to dictate to the defense what the defense can do on a given down and distance, especially on first and second down.
- When the offense varies its substitutions with an assortment of different personnel groupings (e.g., two tight ends, three/four wide receivers, standard), the defense will be put in a position of constantly having to try to keep up with the offense's adjustments.

Diagrams 3-1 through 3-9 show examples of personnel groups using playing card terms. Diagrams 3-10 through 3-15 illustrate two-back sets using standard personnel. In these diagrams, color denotes the formation (empty backfield = fruit term) and right/left designates the strength call (alignment of Y). Only right strength is shown in the diagrams. Many of the formations shown can be aligned to use various personnel groupings. One-back sets are illustrated in Diagrams 3-16 through 3-21 and empty backfield sets are shown in Diagrams 3-22 through 3-25.

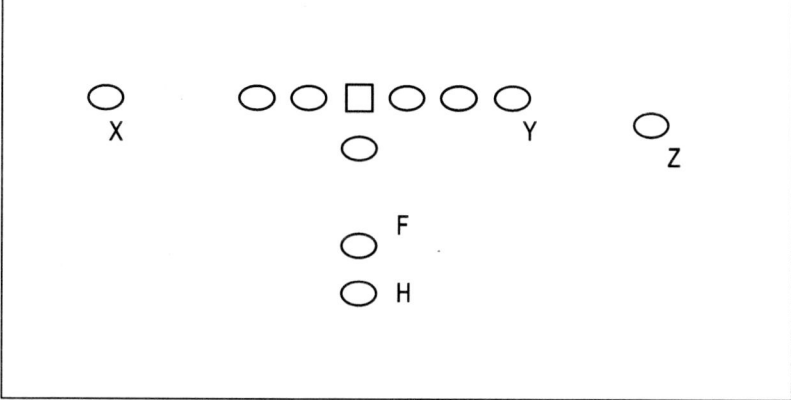

Diagram 3-1. Standard personnel group

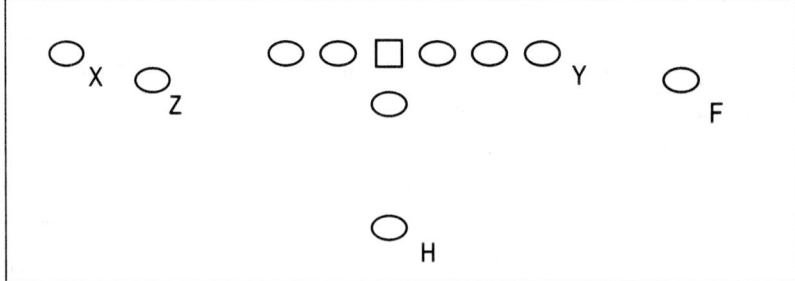

Diagram 3-2. Diamond personnel group

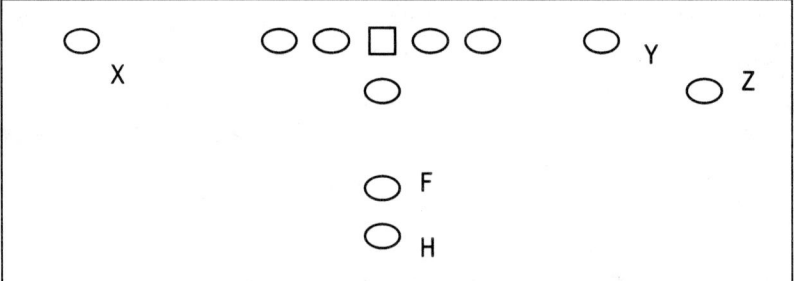

Diagram 3-3. Queens personnel group

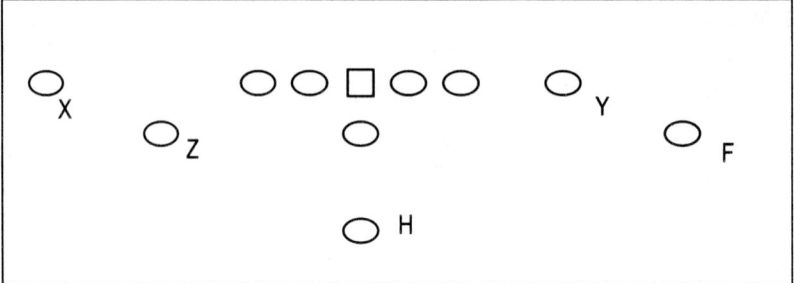

Diagram 3-4. Flush personnel group

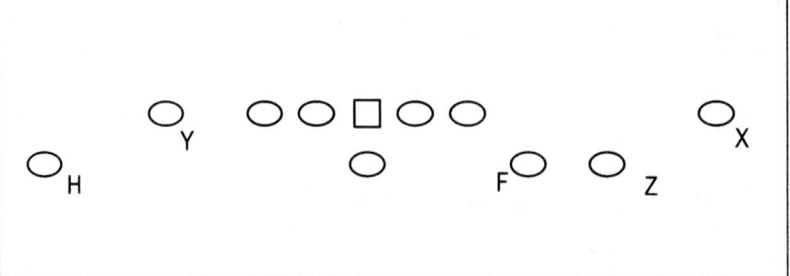

Diagram 3-5. Fives personnel group

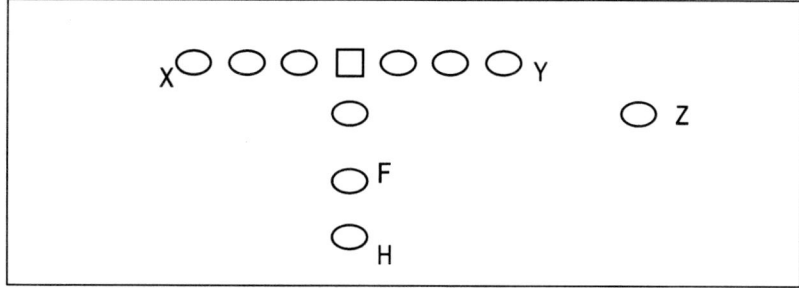

Diagram 3-6. Tens personnel group

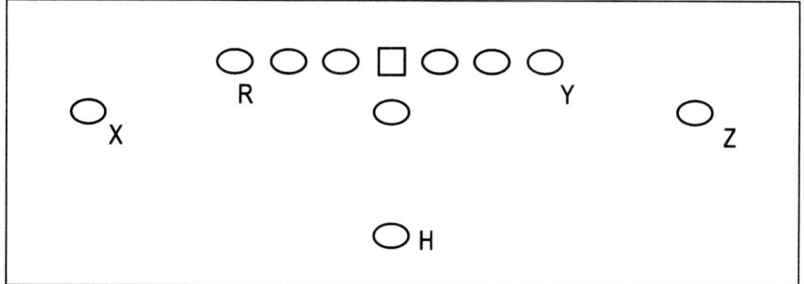

Diagram 3-7. Ace personnel group

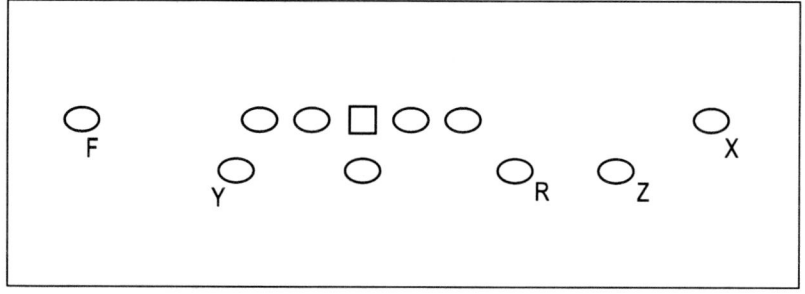

Diagram 3-8. Kings personnel group

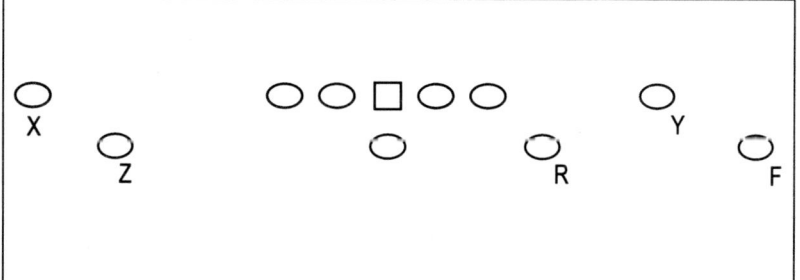

Diagram 3-9. Jacks personnel group

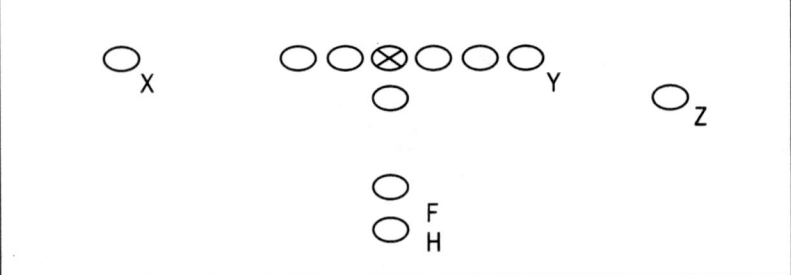
Diagram 3-10. Black right

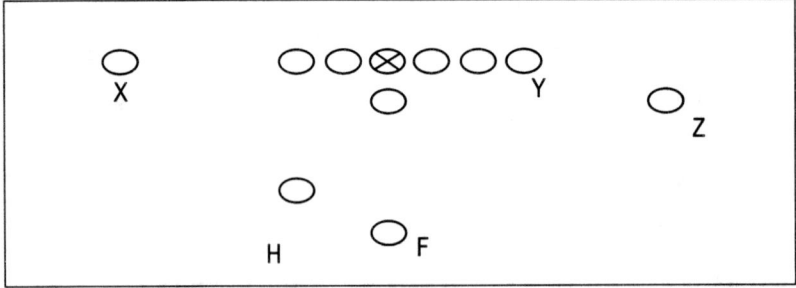
Diagram 3-11. Brown right

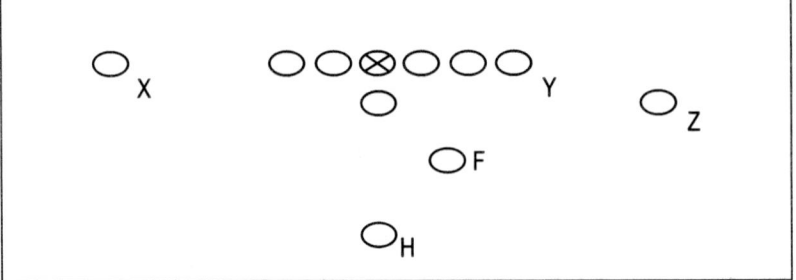
Diagram 3-12. Tan right

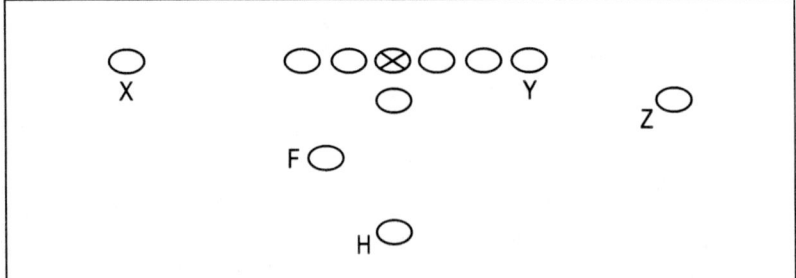
Diagram 3-13. White right

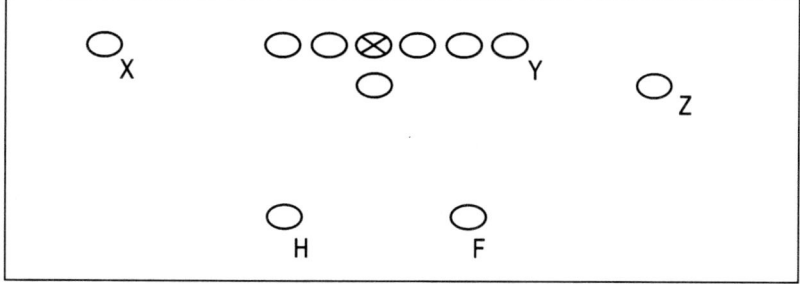

Diagram 3-14. Red right

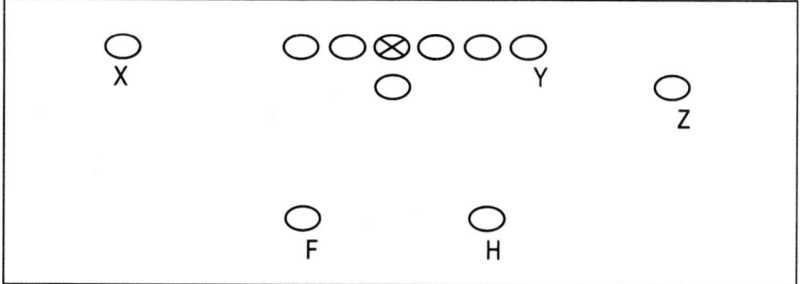

Diagram 3-15. Green right

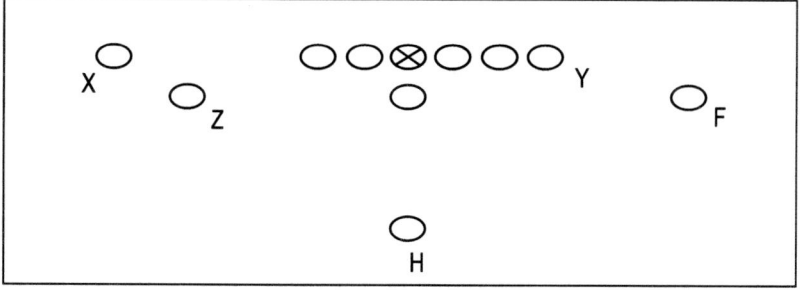

Diagram 3-16. Purple right (diamond)

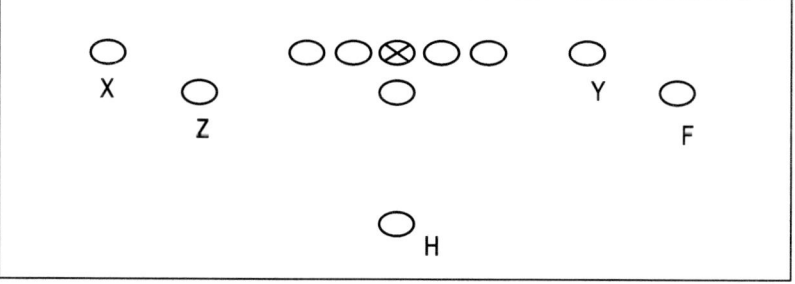

Diagram 3-17. Purple right (flush)

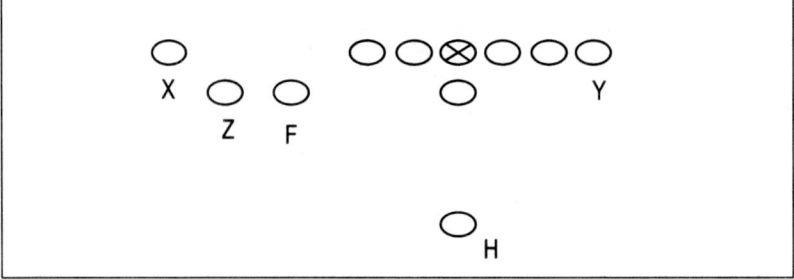
Diagram 3-18. Gold right (diamond)

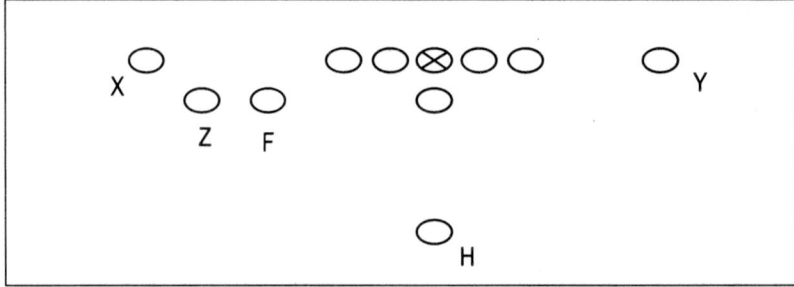
Diagram 3-19. Gold right (flush)

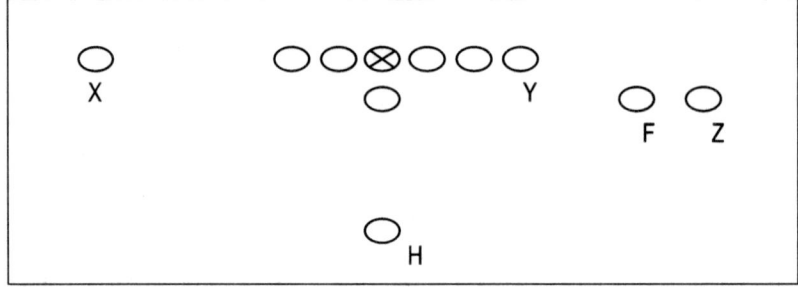
Diagram 3-20. Bronze right (diamond)

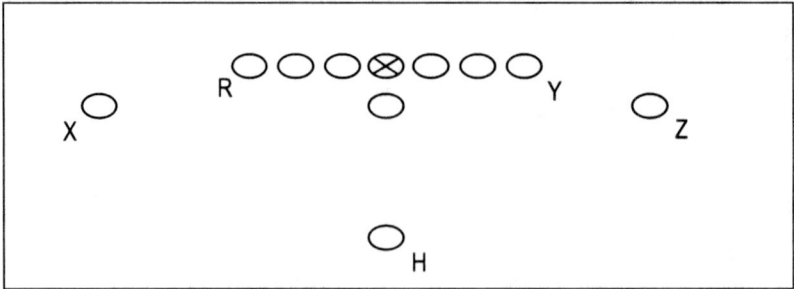
Diagram 3-21. Ace right (ace)

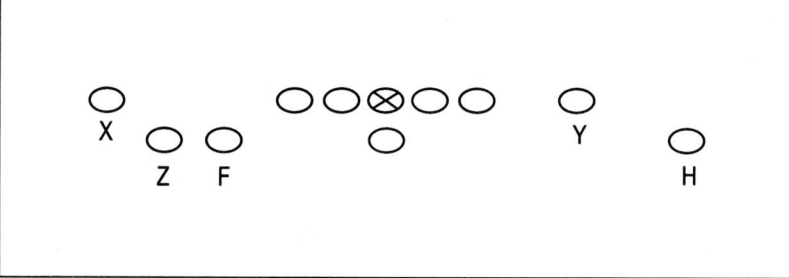

Diagram 3-22. Tangerine right (fives)

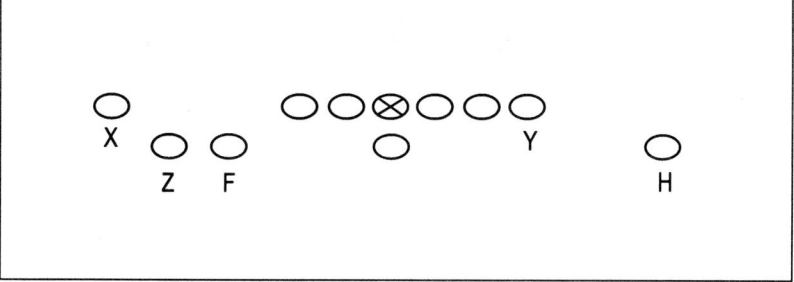

Diagram 3-23. Tangerine right (jacks)

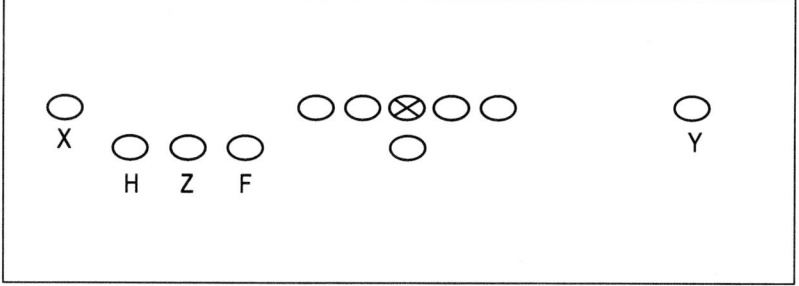

Diagram 3-24. Banana right (fives)

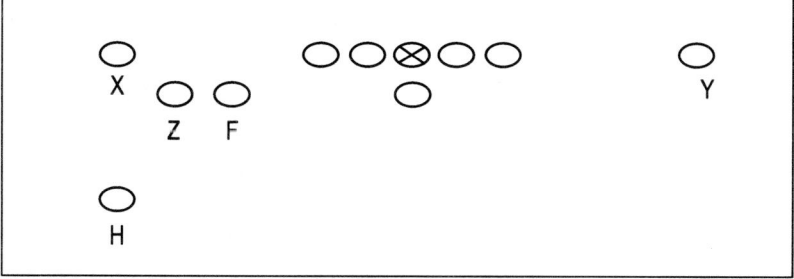

Diagram 3-25. Banana right stack (fives)

49

Key "buzz" words may be added to a formation call to add to an offensive system, making it appear very sophisticated.
- Formations can be aligned from various personnel groupings.
- Motioning and shifting to formations will cause delayed recognition or confusion for many defenses.

Some teams will have a gifted halfback (H) who will not only be a great ballcarrier, but also an exceptional player out in space. The following procedure will help in simplifying the offensive system to allow this exceptional athlete to be moved around.

Adjustments by Halfback

Key terms (Diagram 3-26) will help the offense be more flexible without adding new formations. Refer to Diagrams 3-27 and 3-28 for examples.

LEFT	RIGHT
D = Attached	C = Attached
E = Beyond	B = Beyond
F = Completely Outside	A = Completely Outside

```
         ○○⊗○○
F   E   D   ○   C   B   A
```

NOTE: H will be off the LOS on all of these adjustments.

Diagram 3-26. Adjustments by halfback

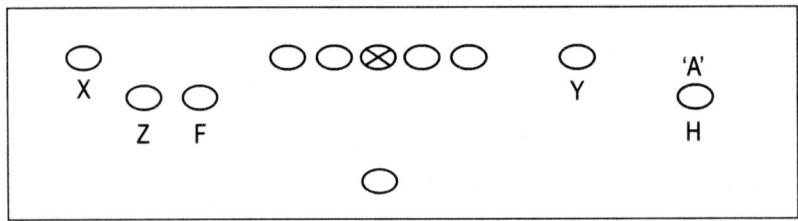

Diagram 3-27. (Flush) Gold right 'A' (empty set)

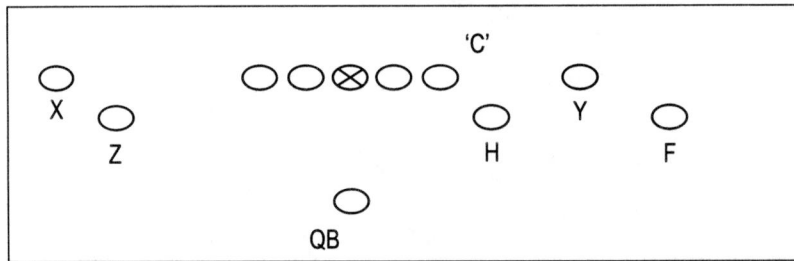

Diagram 3-28. (Flush) Purple right 'C' (builds empty set)

Pre-Snap Movement

All shifting should be done in a crisp, precise manner. The player(s) will shift on the "set" command. All players must be set for one second before the snap of the ball.

Shift: Refers only to the running backs. This is the simplest form of all pre-snap movement. The shifting will be random or by game plan.

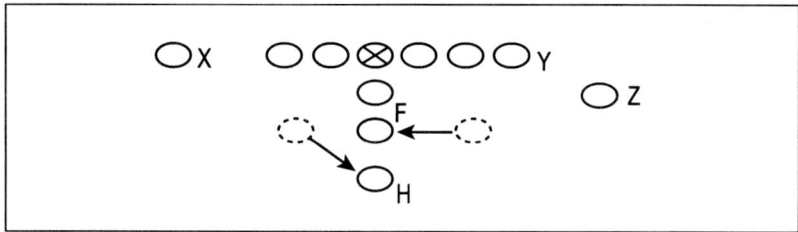

Diagram 3-29. Shift

Trade: Refers to the tight end. May also apply to the running backs, and is based on the game plan.
- The tight end will use the step-off method to ensure a defensive adjustment. Reminder: The wide receivers must be alert to use proper hitching techniques on/off the line of scrimmage.
- The running back(s) will adjust their backfield alignment based on the game plan in a crisp, precise manner.

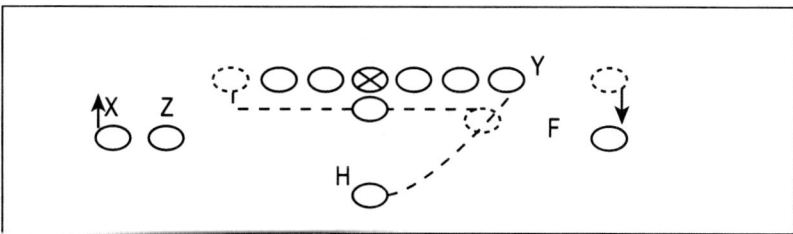

Diagram 3-30. Trade to Purple right

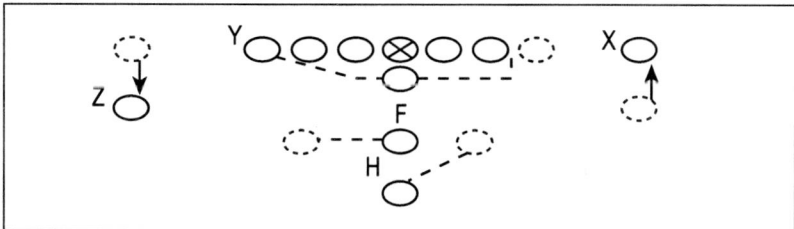

Diagram 3-31. Trade to Black left

Scramble: Designates a random shift by the entire offensive unit. Basic parameters should be given before each game to ensure defensive confusion. Note: Utilize a quick cadence, but make sure all offensive personnel are set for one count prior to the snap.

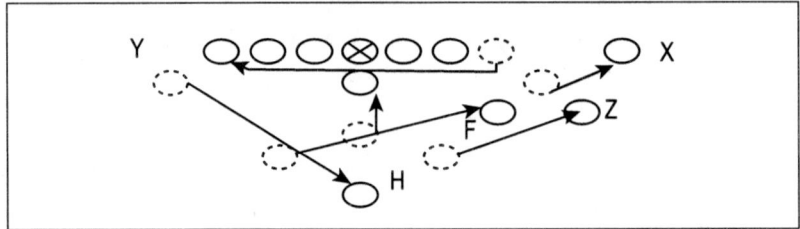

Diagram 3-32. Scramble to Gold left

Mix: A predetermined motion and shift on the same play. Note: The shift will be on the "set" command; the motion will follow by the quarterback's foot (heel) signal. After the shift, the entire offensive unit must be set for one second prior to beginning the motion.

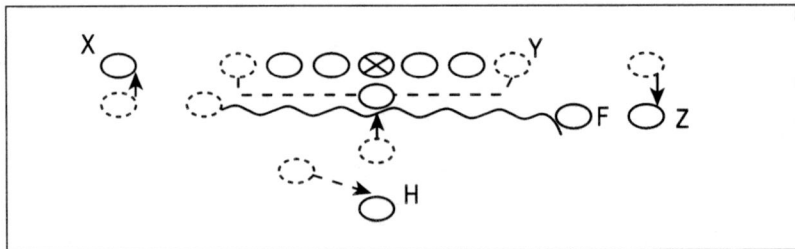

Diagram 3-33. Mix to Bronze right

Motion

The quarterback will call the type of motion in the huddle. The motion will begin by the quarterback moving his foot (heel) or arm (when in gun formation). All players must be set for one second prior to sending the man in motion. The motion should be at a steady pace to allow the quarterback to snap the ball at the proper time. The motion man should be where he is supposed to be when the ball is snapped. Motion is *off* on any audible.

Flanker (Z) Motion: Flanker will use flat motion or may come from the backfield depending on the game plan.

ZOOM—Flanker will motion across the ball.

ZING—Flanker will motion inside but will not cross the ball.

ZORRO—Flanker will motion behind the quarterback and then return to his original alignment.

ZAC—Flanker will motion away from the ball.

ZIP—Flanker will motion across the ball to a tight position outside the weak offensive tackle.

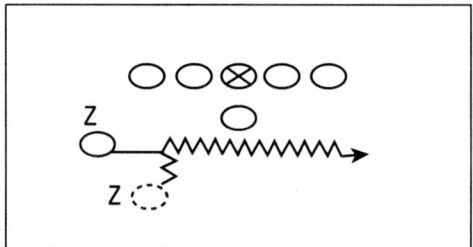
Diagram 3-34. ZOOM motion

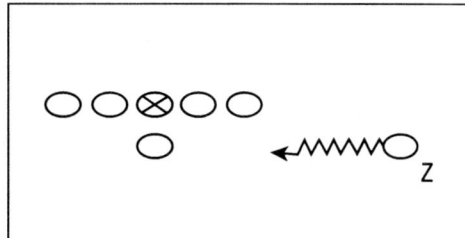
Diagram 3-35. ZING motion

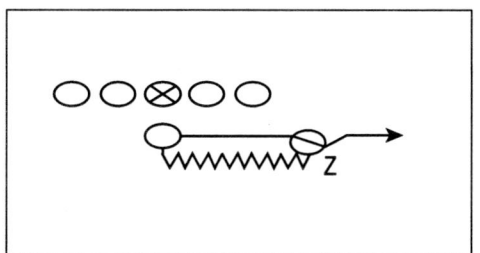
Diagram 3-36. ZORRO motion

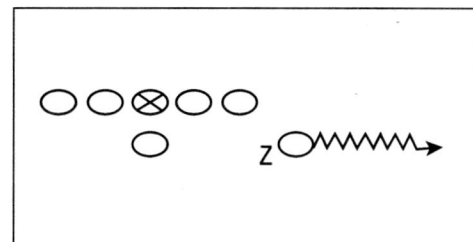
Diagram 3-37. ZAC motion

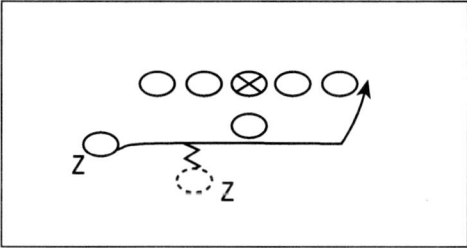
Diagram 3-38. ZIP motion

Tight End (Y) Motion:

YO—Tight end will motion across the ball.

YIN—Tight end will motion inside but not across the ball.

YOYO—Tight end will motion over the ball (behind the quarterback) and return to his original spot.

YAZ—Tight end will motion away from the ball.

Step off motion will be utilized except for during YIN motion. The flanker (Z) must be alert to be on the line of scrimmage after the tight end steps off. The tight end will step off on "set," then will go in motion on the quarterback's foot (heel) movement. The tight end will begin motion from various locations (based on the play or game plan).

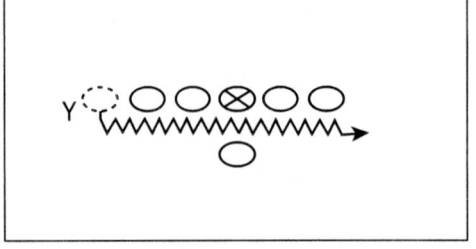

Diagram 3-39. YO motion

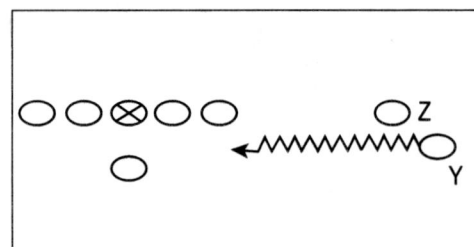

Diagram 3-40. YIN motion

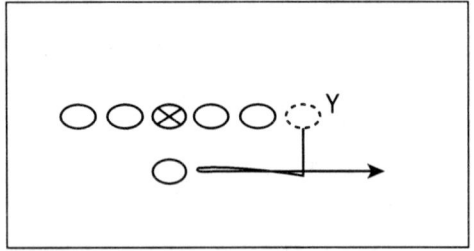

Diagram 3-41. YOYO motion

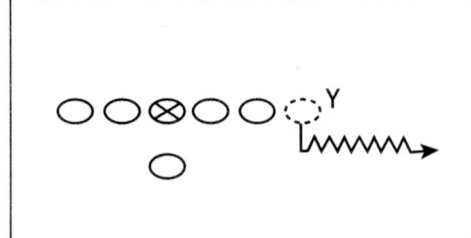

Diagram 3-42. YAZ motion

Wide Receiver (F) Motion:

Fly—Motion begins from various locations and always crosses the ball.

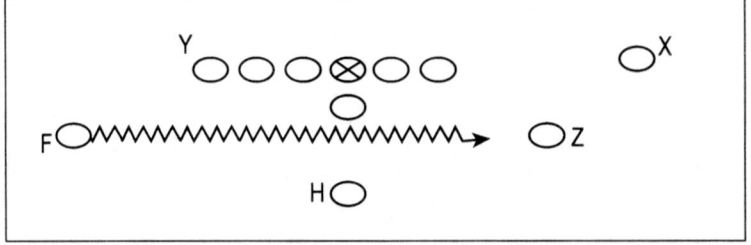

Diagram 3-43. Fly to Gold left

FOB (F orbit)—Motion to behind the quarterback and then return to the original alignment.

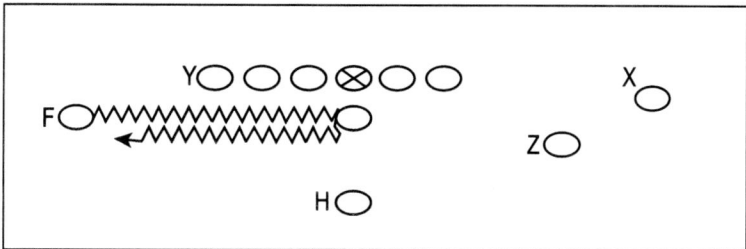

Diagram 3-44. FOB motion

Running Back Motion from the Backfield

Fullback (F) Motion From the Backfield:

FOY—Fullback motion to the tight end (Y) side

FOX—Fullback motion to the split end (X) side

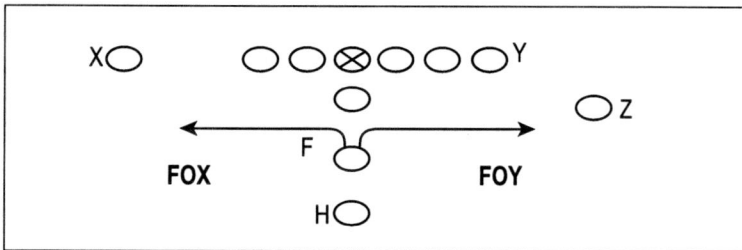

Diagram 3-45. FOX and FOY motion

Halfback (H) motion from the backfield to empty formation. Motion can be to either the A or F (halfback) locations.

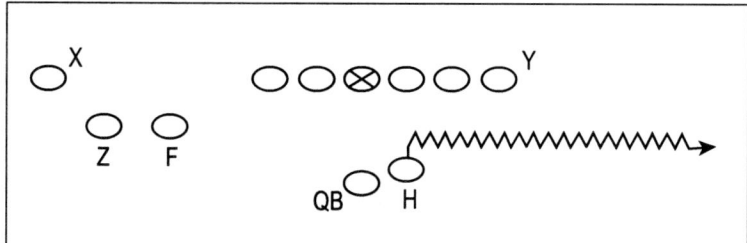

Diagram 3-46. Motion to Gold right 'A'

Split End (X) motion across the ball. This is usually used to build an unbalanced formation alignment.

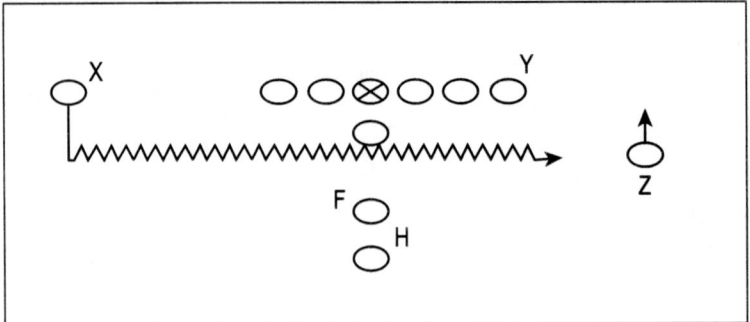

Diagram 3-47. Jet-Split end (X) motion

4

The Passing Game

When developing a passing game, it is important to design one that the players can execute. "Keep it simple" is a great motto. The players need to understand the terminology so that they can make the correct reads and adjustments. It is also important to build a system that fits your players' abilities and gets the best 11 players on the field. Remember: *A style of your own*.

The quarterback is the most important element in an explosive offense. Therefore, the passing philosophy should be flexible and broad enough to fit the ability level of the quarterback. It is always best to adjust the system to the abilities of the quarterback, rather than try to adjust the quarterback to the system. The same offense can be run with either the mobile quarterback or the dropback quarterback. The only needed change is to emphasize the set-up or launch points that suit the skills of the quarterback.

Factors to consider when developing an explosive offense:
- Some teams may not have the manpower or resources to compete with more talented teams. A well-conceived passing attack will help a team equalize some of these differences.

- The passing game provides opportunities for players to individually develop their skills. For example, quarterbacks and receivers can be involved in summer passing leagues to further develop their talents.
- The passing game should force the defense to defend the entire football field. Defenses usually utilize three main types of secondary coverages to defend against the pass.
    - ✓ Zone—defenders are responsible for certain areas of the field
    - ✓ Man—defenders are assigned specific receivers to defend/cover
    - ✓ Combo—a combination of man and zone coverage
- The passing game allows the offense to utilize different formations, personnel groupings, and motions to isolate one-on-one situations and create mismatches in personnel. For example, you can isolate a quick running back on a linebacker, or a fast wide receiver on a strong safety.
- The better a team becomes at throwing the football, the more success they will have at running the football. This happens because the defense will deploy their defenders to stop the pass, thus opening up more opportunities to run the ball.
- The passing game is the best means of attacking the defense when in a long yardage situation.
- By using the total package of the passing game (e.g., quick passes, dropback, sprint-out, play-action, screens, draws), the offense can maintain possession of the ball and achieve ball control.

The underlying philosophy of a successful passing attack is *commitment*. Total commitment and dedication to the passing game will ensure ample time to practice the techniques necessary for success. Players should also believe that they can win by throwing the football—from anywhere on the field and at any time during the game.

Evaluating Personnel

It is important to evaluate all of the offensive positions, not just the quarterback. This will help blend your players' strengths to get 11 individuals executing as a unit.

Once you have evaluated each of your players, it is very important to make sure that all players are taught the proper fundamentals needed to play their positions at a high level. Fundamentals are the key to success. Many coaches place scheme before fundamentals. A team will not be successful doing this. Each position coach should have a list of drills that will be utilized when coaching his position.

Offensive Linemen

Assess overall ability to determine pass protection schemes to utilize. Examples include three- and five- step (dropback), sprint, and play-action.

Running Backs/Tight Ends

These positions are the easiest to get open in a passing game. A thorough evaluation will get the most out of their talent.

Wide Receivers

Evaluate the overall athletic ability of these players (e.g., quickness, speed, agility, catching ability). Make sure to use the receivers' strengths. Design routes and patterns that feature an individual receiver's capabilities.

Quarterback Launch Points

An effective passing game should have precision. The quarterback should set up at specific depths/locations and release the ball on time.

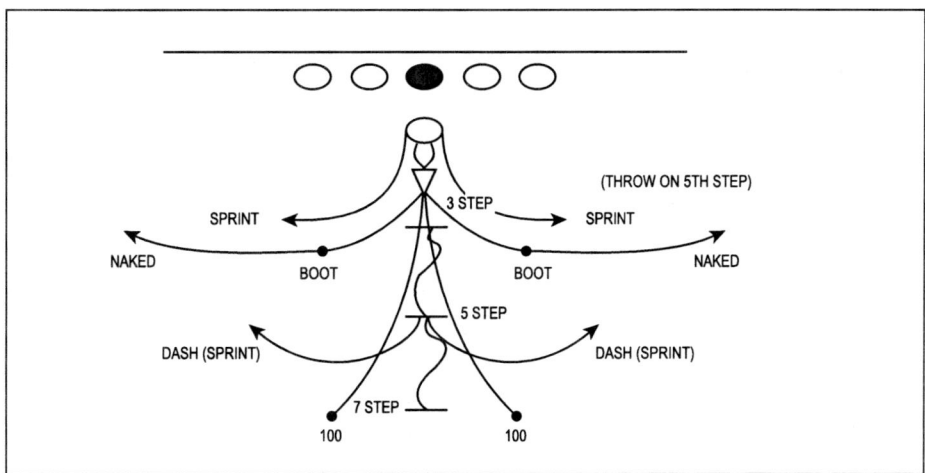

Diagram 4-1. Quarterback launch points

Quarterback Underneath-the-Center Set-Up and Timing

- 3-step: Three-to-four yards (.9 seconds)
- 5-step (quick): Five yards (1.3 seconds)
- 5-step (regular): Six-to-seven yards (hitch forward) (1.5 seconds)
- 7-step (gun): Nine-to-10 yards (hitch forward) (1.75 seconds)

Quarterback Gun Alignment

- 3-step pass: Secure ball-snap throw
- 5-step pass: Rhythm steps only
- 7-step pass: 3-step drop after receiving gun snap

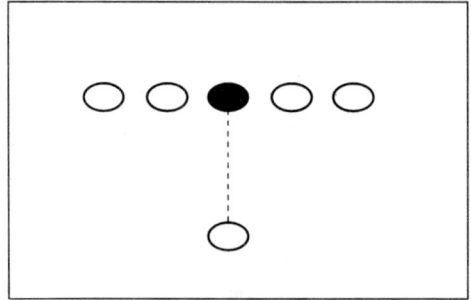

Diagram 4-2. Quarterback gun alignment

Route Trees

Wide Receiver Route Tree

Refer to Diagram 4-3.

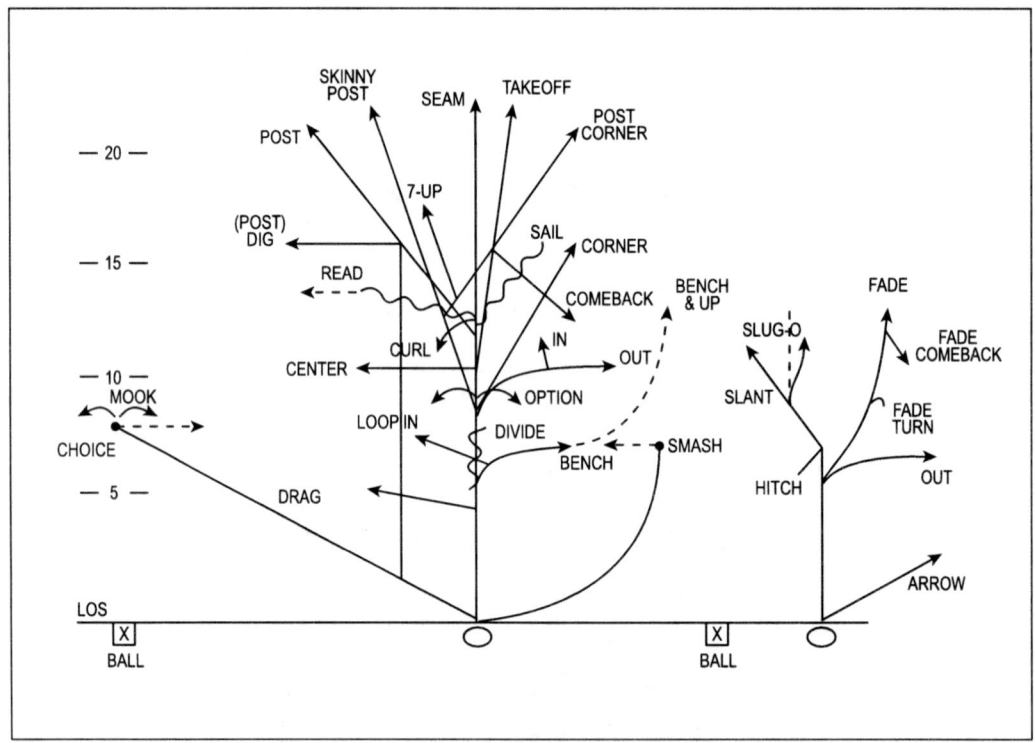

Diagram 4-3. Wide receiver route tree

Tight End Route Tree

The tight end is responsible for executing all wide receiver routes when placed in wide-open (i.e., spread) formations.

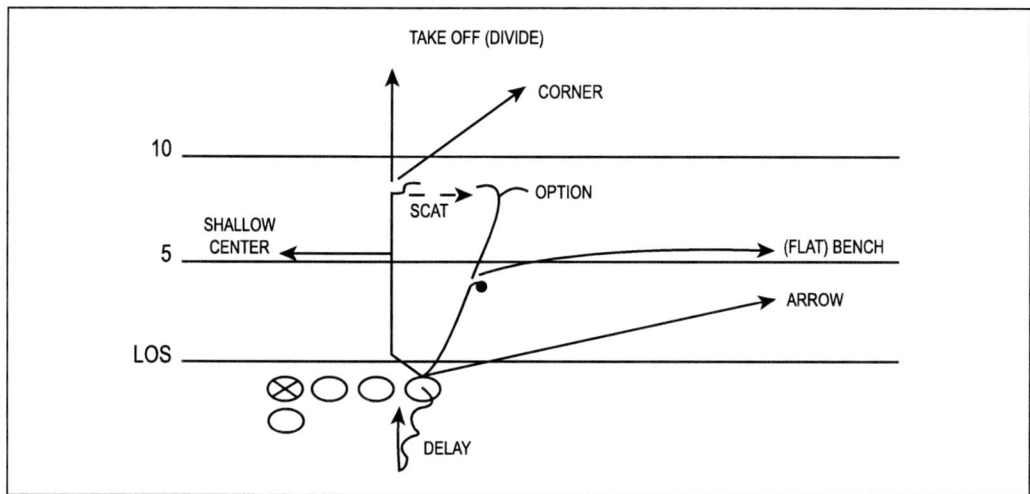

Diagram 4-4. Tight end route tree

Running Back Route Tree

The running back may be designated a *hot* receiver on various pass routes. Also, the running backs are responsible for executing all wide receiver routes when placed in wide-open (i.e., spread) formations.

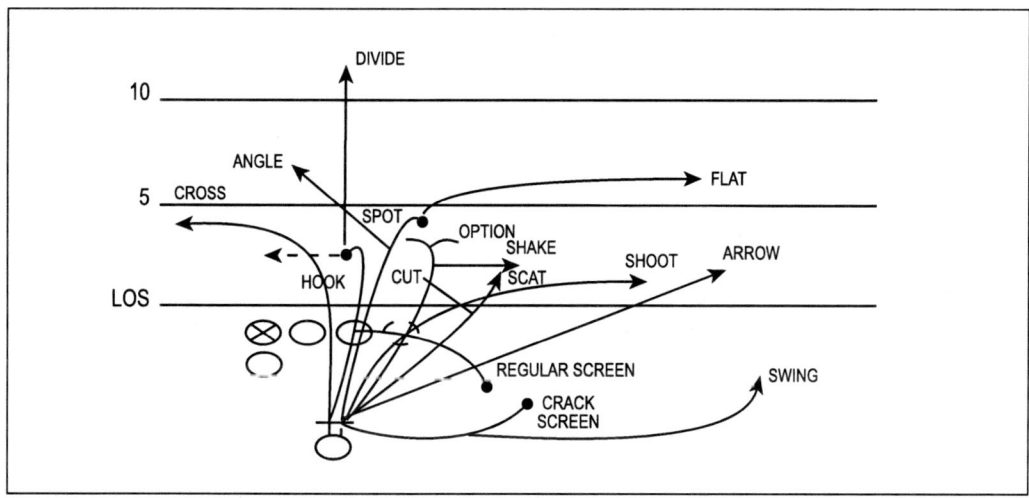

Diagram 4-5. Running back route tree

Quarterback Drops/Individual Routes

The following outline will provide a basic understanding of how the quarterback's drop and the receiver's route should go hand in hand to create smoothness in the passing game. (Refer to route trees).

With a three-step drop, the set-up goal is .9 seconds. Example routes include:
- Quick hitch
- Quick slant
- Quick out
- Arrow
- Goal line fade

With a five-step drop, the set-up goal is 1.3 seconds. Example routes include:
- Out
- Smash
- Choice
- Option
- Takeoff (seam)
- Skinny post
- Drag
- Cross
- Bench
- Scat (tight end)
- Corner drag
- Sail
- Dig

Various routes can be executed out of gun. The quarterback will receive the ball from a five-yard depth, then take rhythm steps. The quarterback will take the ball from gun, then take a normal three-step drop to help the timing of the routes.

With a seven-step drop, the set-up goal is 1.75 seconds. These routes are deeper (down the field), and therefore take more time to develop. The quarterback may also utilize gun alignment to execute these routs. Example routes include:
- In
- Post
- Post cross
- Post corner

Running Back Routes

For simplicity, the quarterback should take a five-step drop, look down the field, and then progress down to throw to the running back. Exceptions: possible hot throws when the running back releases quickly into the pattern with no pass protection responsibility.

When designing pass patterns, it is important to remember that the quarterback drops (set-up) and the individual routes must complement each other. This allows the offense to flow with the ball delivered on time. Diagrams 4-6 through 4-8 illustrate common timing and routes.

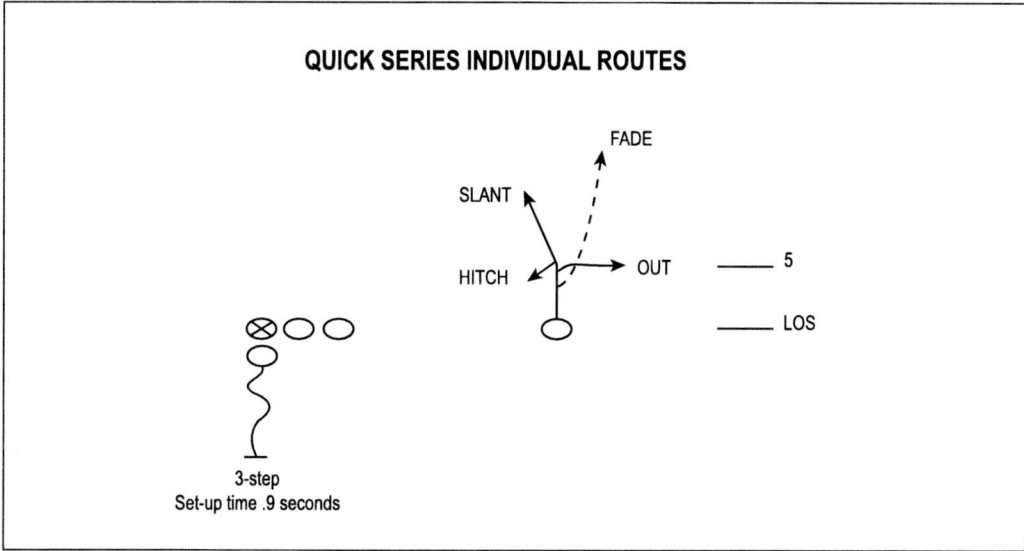

Diagram 4-6. Three-step (quick series) timing and routes

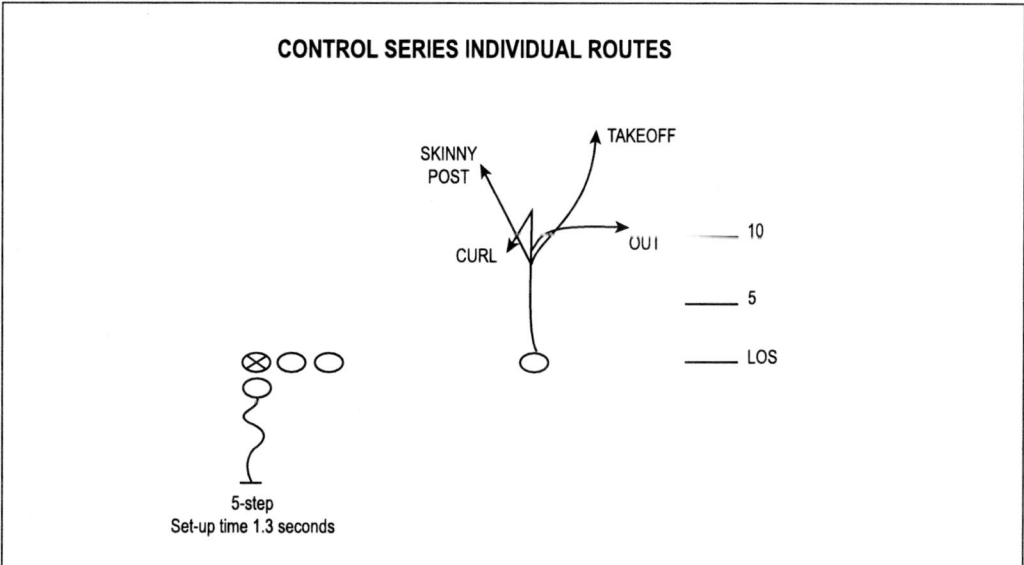

Diagram 4-7. Five-step (controlled passes) timing and routes

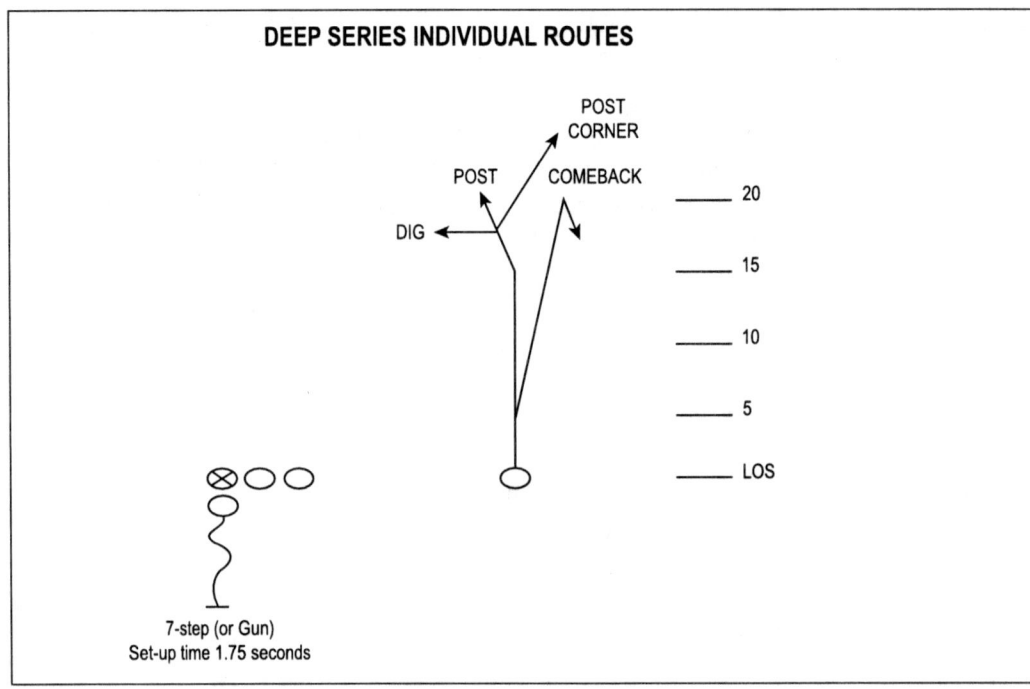

Diagram 4-8. Seven-step gun (down the field) timing and routes

Practicing the Passing Game

When implementing the passing game, it is important to practice it in proper progression. Diagram 4-9 shows the base progression that should be used during practices.

Practice Progressions to Develop the Passing Game	
Skill Positions	Offensive Line Protections
• Fundamentals	• Fundamentals
• Individual Routes vs. Air	• Combo Drills (1/1; Twists/Stunts)
• Man/Man vs Defense	• 5 vs. 4 (Pass Rush)
• 5 vs. Air (patterns)	• Blitz Pick-Up (include RB's/TE)
• Pass Skeleton	• Team Pass/Blitz
• Team Pass/Blitz	

Diagram 4-9. Practice progressions to develop the passing game

Basic Practice Format

Warm-up

The individual warm-up period is directed by the position coach. This will include very light agility drills that relate to an individual's particular position. This segment is followed by a team stretch.

Fundamentals

Fundamentals are the key to success. Fundamentals should be practiced every day. A position coach should utilize a variety of drills to enhance a player's attitude toward practicing fundamentals. It is important that each position coach is very demanding during this phase of practice and encourages the players to strive for perfection on every repetition.

Skill and Technique Work

Each position coach should identify the skills and techniques the players need to develop to do their assignment. The drills should fit within the offense's existing system.

Group Drills

The two basic types of group drills are competition and scout team. Competitive drills involve bringing two groups together to work against each other in a competitive environment. Examples include pass skeleton (seven-on-seven), inside run, and man-to-man. Scout team drills are instructional in nature. One group of players is used to service the needs of the other group.

Team Drills

Two complete units of the team are brought together to work competitively against each other, or as a scout team to each other. In most situations, it is important to script the play, down/distance, hash, and field location. This will help the coaches evaluate the offense's execution of the play.

Wide Receiver Fundamentals and Drills

The following fundamentals and drills can be applied to all offensive skill positions—wide receiver, tight end, and running back.

Catching the Football

- Make the routine catch

- Make the tough catch
- Get yards after the catch

Catching the football requires concentration and dedication. A wide receiver can never catch enough balls. Repetition, repetition, repetition. The more balls a player catches, the more natural it will become. Catching the football should be a natural reaction.

The wide receiver should "look the ball into his hands." The last 12 inches of the flight of the football are the most important. It is at this point that many wide receivers take their eyes off the ball and drop it. Remind your players that a great throw, protection, and route are all wasted if the ball is not caught.

General principles of catching the ball:
- If the ball is above the waist, the thumbs should be in. If the ball is below the waist, the thumbs should be out.
- Catch the ball out in front by extending the arms.
- The hands and fingers should be relaxed and give with the ball.
- The catch is not complete until the ball is put away.
- On high throws, get the fingers over the top of the point, so if the ball is not caught cleanly, it will fall downward and give the receiver a second shot.
- On over-the-shoulder throws, keep the elbows in to form a cradle and see the ball all the way into the catch.
- On underthrown balls to outs, curls, or digs, slow down to let the ball come to the front number. Try not to reach back.
- On the underthrown deep ball, come back and catch the ball at its highest point.
- On the low-thrown ball, get the fingers and palms under the ball. Keep the elbows in.

Fingertip Drills (to develop strong fingertips)

- Push-ups (five for every drop)
- Hand flip—Flip the ball back and forth without losing contact with it
- Air dribble—"Dribble" the ball without dropping it on the ground
- Around/figure-eight—Grip and re-grip the ball around the body or do figure-eights through the legs as quickly as possible
- Tug-o-war—Two receivers grab opposite points of the ball and play tug-o-war

Basic Pass-Catching Drills

> Motto: Receivers will make the tough catches look routine, and will make the impossible catches possible, through a little extra practice. Make the big play!

Catch and Tuck

Objective: This drill is the most elementary of all pass-catching drills. The quarterback will warm up his arm while working on accuracy. The receiver will emphasize catching the ball with his fingertips (or "eyes"), then tucking the ball away properly.

Description: The quarterback and receiver will position themselves approximately 10 yards apart.

Turn

Objective: To emphasize accuracy—the ball should be delivered exactly on the jersey number. The receiver will learn to snap his head around quickly to pick up the flight of the ball, tuck it away, and advance the ball down the field.

Description: The receiver will be positioned 10 yards from the quarterback, facing in the opposite direction. On the quarterback's command, the receiver will quickly throw his elbow, (in the direction he is going to break), snap his head around to pick up the flight of the ball, catch the ball (with his hands), tuck it away (away from defense), and advance the ball up the field (while making a move).

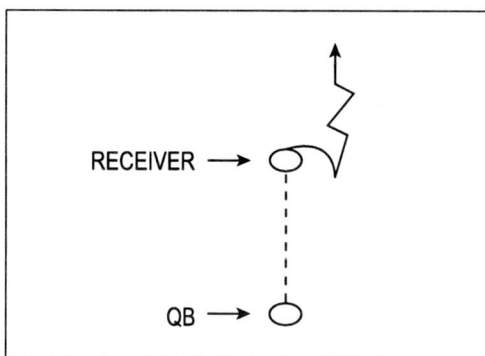

Diagram 4-10. Turn drill

Turn and Go

Objective: To improve the quarterback's accuracy while throwing to the receiver on the move. The first phase of this drill is the same as the turn drill, but as the receiver throws his arm, he sprints down the line (staying on it until the catch is made), then tucks it away, and advances toward the goal line.

Description: The quarterback and receiver will be in a staggered alignment (simulating the last phase of an out route) approximately five to 10 yards apart. The quarterback gives either a "turn" or "go" command. This drill should be practiced in both directions.

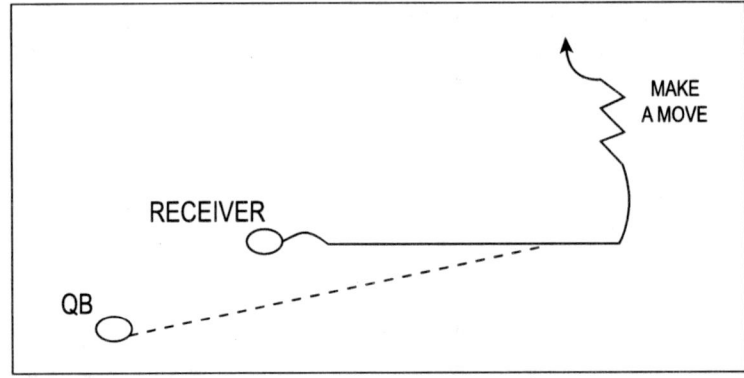

Diagram 4-11. Turn and go drill

Last Phase of a Curl

Objective: To teach the receiver to come back to the ball and meet it, then transfer his weight to advance the ball upfield.

Description: The quarterback will slightly stagger the receiver's position 10 yards away. On the "go" command, the quarterback will execute a three-step drop; the receiver will accelerate three steps, then complete the last phase of a curl (coming slightly inside from his initial stem). This drill should be practiced in both directions.

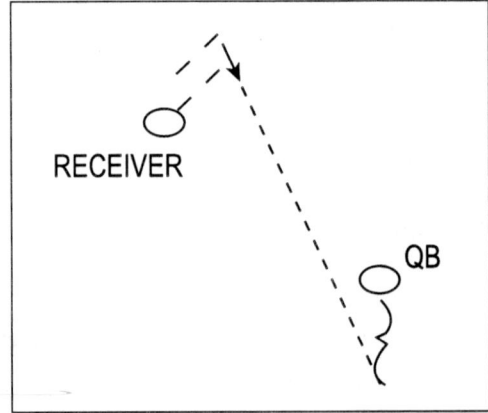

Diagram 4-12. Last phase of a curl drill

Blaster

Objective: To teach the receiver to make the catch, knowing he is going to get hit. This develops mental toughness and concentration.

Description: The quarterback will throw the ball in between two defenders. When the ball passes the defenders, they "blast" the receiver with the pads, trying to knock the ball loose. The receiver moves his feet, makes the catch, and puts the ball away. The turn drill can also be added.

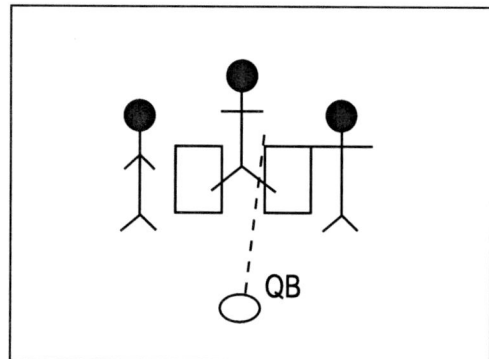

Diagram 4-13. Blaster drill

Blur

Objective: To teach the quarterback to throw accurately as a defender moves in front of the receiver. The receiver will learn to concentrate on the flight of the ball, catch it, and tuck it away.

Description: Position two lines of receivers approximately 10 to 15 yards apart. One line of receivers is one yard off of the line of scrimmage. On the "go" command, both receivers will run on their path—one as a receiver, one as a defender (blur action). The football should be thrown at the mesh point. This drill should be practiced in both directions.

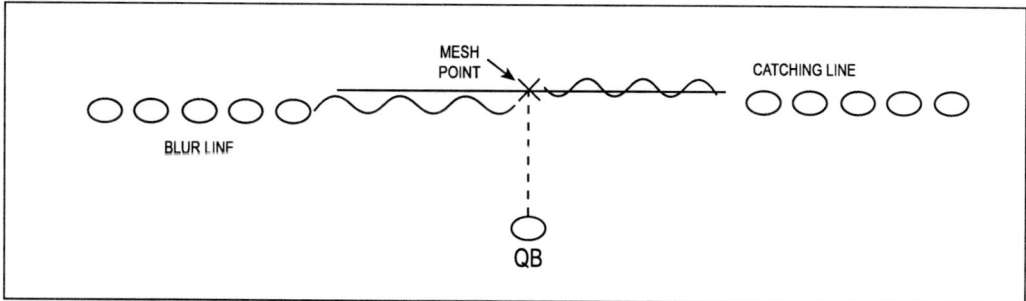

Diagram 4-14. Blur drill

Pat-n-Go

Objective: This is an easy-paced warm-up for both the quarterback and receivers.

Description: Two lines of receivers are aligned on the field hash marks. The distances may vary. The receivers will rotate after the catch to the next line going in the opposite direction (this will help save the legs). Alternate the direction and the type of catches.

Phases:
- Both hands
- One hand
- Tip and catch

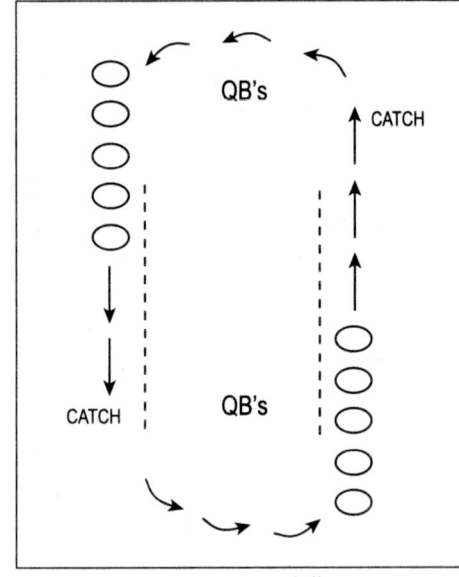

Diagram 4-15. Pat-n-go drill

Highest Point

Objective: To teach the receiver to come back for an underthrown football and catch it at its highest point.

Description: The quarterback underthrows the receiver on a fade route. The receiver should stop, come back, and jump up to catch the ball at its highest point.

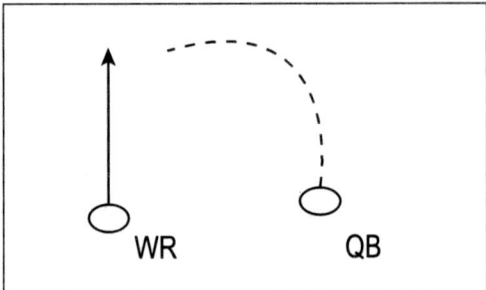

Diagram 4-16. Highest point drill

Defender

Objective: To teach the receiver to become a defensive back when the ball is about to be intercepted.

Description: The quarterback underthrows the fade route to the inside. When the receiver recognizes that the ball is going to be intercepted, he goes up and knocks the ball away from the defender.

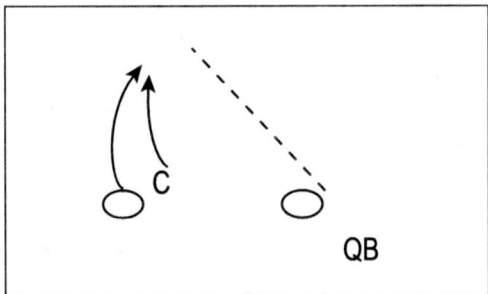

Diagram 4-17. Defender drill

Sideline

Objective: To develop footwork for the receivers as they are making a touch catch on the sideline.

Description: The receiver executes a four-to-six yard speed break out, snaps his head around, and makes the catch with the hands while keeping both feet inbounds. Receivers should alternate lines after each catch.

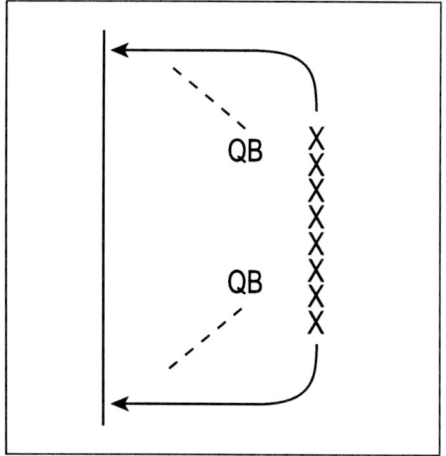

Diagram 4-18. Sideline drill

Tightrope

Objective: To teach the receivers to stay inbounds when possible after a sideline catch to strive for extra yards.

Description: Same as the sideline drill, except the receiver will "tightrope" the sideline to get a first down. Receivers should alternate lines after each catch.

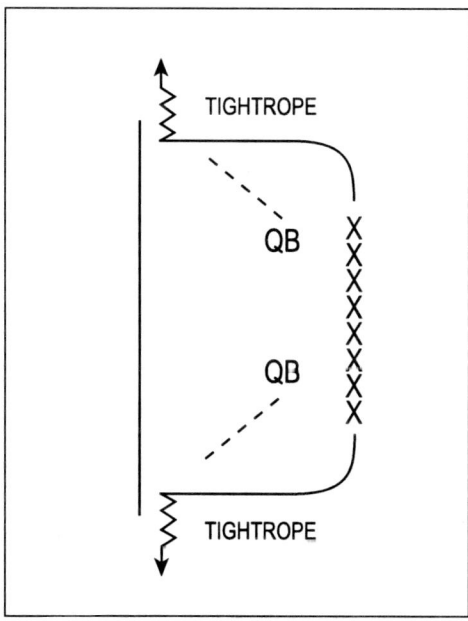

Diagram 4-19. Tightrope drill

Dive

Objective: To teach the receiver to lay out for the ball and maintain concentration.

Description: The receiver will run and lay out for the ball. The quarterback should throw the ball to time the receiver's jump.

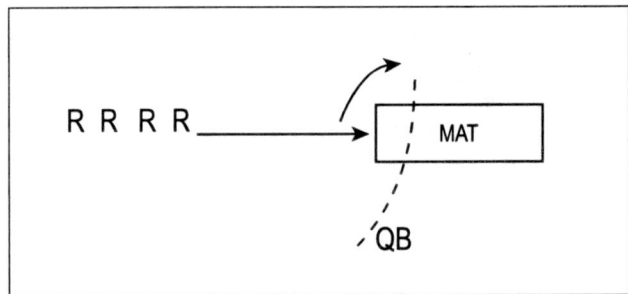

Diagram 4-20. Dive drill

Wiffle Balls

Wiffle ball drills can be used year-round to develop hand/eye coordination.

Jug Machine

Receivers should run the last phase of routes and catch lots of balls off the jug machine. The jug machine throws a steady, consistent ball, which will allow the receivers to get lots of repetitions.

Route Running

Four Keys to Good Route Running

Speed

Speed off the ball (passes and runs) is only one of the essential types of speed. Speed in and out of breaks and knowing when to fluctuate speeds are also vitally important.

Leverage

It is very important to get leverage on the defensive back, especially versus man coverage. Leverage is gained by working for a head-up position on the defender. For example, during an out route versus a defender in an off, outside technique, the receiver should try to get leverage by stemming to a head-up position on the defender. Stemming:

- Can occur off the line or downfield.
- Will help get leverage on a defender
- Will help get a tip on the coverage

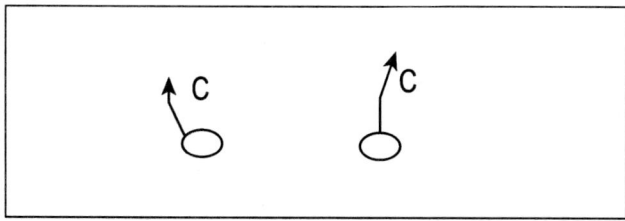

Diagram 4-21. Getting leverage by stemming

Influence

The receiver has the advantage because he knows where he is going. The receiver should turn the hips (i.e., influence) of the defender away from where he intends to make his final break, or before he pressures the defender deep. The influence includes:
- Head fake, jab step, and speed fluctuation
- Creating separation versus man coverage, and air versus zone coverage

Body Control

It is very important that a receiver keep his body under control while running routes, especially when trying to get in and out of break points. Receivers get into trouble when they slow down, rise up, drop their arms to their sides, or run routes with curves and wide arcs. All these things will be picked up by a good defender and will allow him to close the cushion more quickly.

Speed, leverage, and influence will enable a receiver to create separation. By keeping his body under control, the receiver will be able to maintain this separation longer.

Break Point

Objectives

- To gain advantage on the defender
- To increase the distance between the defender and the receiver
- To gain a desired position versus a zone defense
- To decrease the angle of the ball for the receiver while increasing that of defenders
- To gain body position so that the body is between the ball and the defender

- To be at a specific point at a specific time
- To get the defender's body weight leaning backward at the breaking point

Techniques for Receivers

- Create the illusion of going somewhere other than where you end up
- Thrust the head and shoulders forward
- Lower the center of gravity (i.e., sink the hips)
- Keep the arms bent
- Keep the elbows in near the sides of the body and pump them with each step of the opposite foot
- Spread the feet as the center of gravity is lowered, and cut and drive off of the foot opposite the direction of the cut
- Accelerate just prior to the cut to create the illusion that you are going deep
- Cut sharply and whip the head quickly toward the quarterback

Footwork Drills to Aid Receivers in Making Efficient Cuts/Breaks

Refer to Diagrams 4-22 through 4-25.

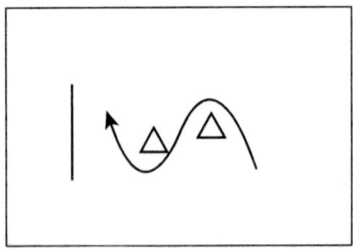

Diagram 4-22. Zag drill

Diagram 4-23. In/out drill

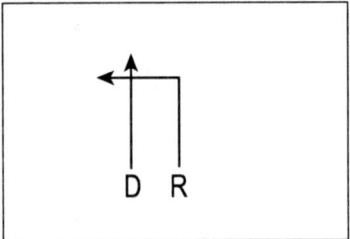

Diagram 4-24. Throw by drill

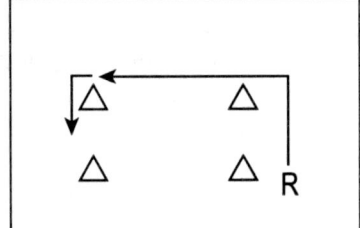

Diagram 4-25. Square drill

Route Guidelines

- Have the receivers run routes that the quarterback can throw consistently.
- Have patterns that work versus everything and patterns designed to defeat certain coverage.

- The number one thing a receiver should understand before becoming a good route runner is defense. This will allow the receiver to know when, where, and how to adjust his route versus certain coverages.

Routes Versus Man Coverage

- Teach the receiver to scare the defender with a move to the area the defender has been told to cover (where he has no help).
- If a defender's technique places him to the side of the intended break, the receiver's move should be a longer one to get the defender turned out of the breaking area.
- If a defender's technique places him opposite the side of the intended route, the receiver should use a smaller move to keep from losing the advantage already gained on the release.
- Versus bump and run, the receiver should release to the side of the cut if possible, but should not sacrifice the ability to get into the secondary. A strong head and shoulder fake opposite the direction of the final cut will be necessary.
- Versus man coverage, the emphasis is on beating the man assigned to cover the receiver.
- Whenever possible, the receiver should create a deep feeling (i.e., illusion of going deep) in the defender's mind.
- Instruct the receivers to make cuts as sharp as possible and accelerate out of the cut to keep the separation already gained.
- Receivers must remember: get leverage, close the cushion, and run by defenders.

Routes Versus Zone Coverage

- The emphasis is on beating the underneath coverage. Teach the receivers to stretch the coverage.
- Most of the man techniques will hold for gaining separation, but after the break it is the receiver's goal to find the holes in the coverage.
- Inside cuts do not have to be made as sharply as the outside cuts.
- Teach the receivers to get the head around quickly to locate the open area when working inside.
- Receivers must be ready to adjust to balls thrown to an open area. This requires them to be a little more under control.
- Receivers must be ready to work back between defenders to the reception spot.

Ball Security

Ball security should be stressed to all receivers. Remind them that a big play can be negated with a fumble. Diagram 4-26 illustrates an effective ball security drill.

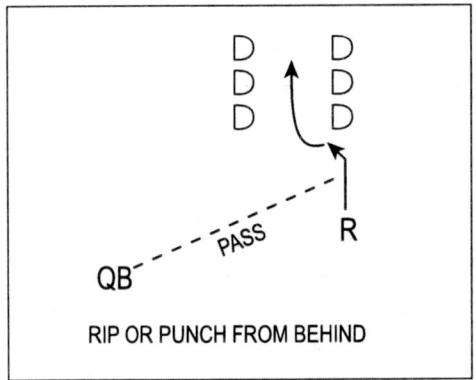

Diagram 4-26. Strip/gauntlet drill

YAC—Yards after Catch or Contact

In any offense, YAC will be crucial to the team's success. Receivers should make people miss. "Turn a five-yard pass into a 20-yard gain!" A useful YAC drill is shown in Diagram 4-27.

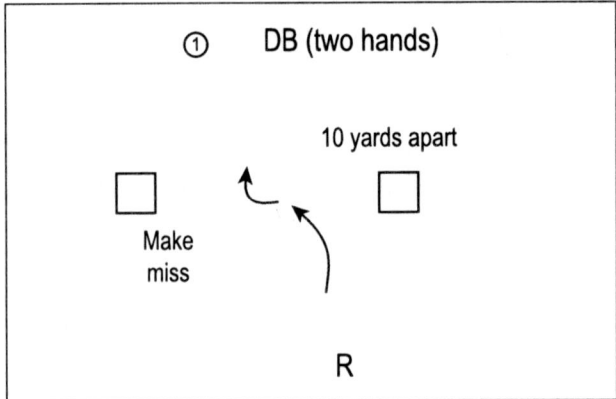

Diagram 4-27. Yards after catch or contact drill

As the passing attack begins to evolve, it is important to challenge the players to take their games to a higher level.

> Motto: Perfection is the goal—but excellence will be tolerated!
> Light up the scoreboard!

5

Protect the Quarterback

When formulating a plan for the passing game, the most important consideration should be protecting the quarterback. For a passing game to be successful, the quarterback must have adequate time to read the defensive pass coverage, pick up the appropriate receiver, and deliver the football. And, the receivers should have time to execute their pass routes. For all of this to be accomplished, the offensive line, running backs, and tight ends must successfully execute their pass protection assignments.

Pass protection needs to be practiced daily. Just as the quarterbacks, receivers, and running backs should work on their individual routes and team patterns, so should the offensive line work daily on improving their individual pass protection skills and protection schemes. The success of any offense is primarily dependent upon the effective performance of the offensive line. Individually and collectively as a unit, the success of the offense is directly affected by their performance. The offensive line has two basic functions of equal importance:
- Keep the defensive rushers away from the passer.
- Open holes for the offensive ballcarriers.

> Motto: When you control the line of scrimmage—you control the ball!
> When you control the ball—you control the score!

Many methods can be used to protect the quarterback, so it is important to select the type(s) that best fit your personnel and can be successfully executed. A few important points to consider:

- Practice protections according to the game plan. Every scheme cannot be given equal repetitions in a practice session. [Example: five-step (40%); three-step (30%); play-action (15%); others—screens, sprint outs, etc. (15%)]
- Defenses can always bring at least one more defender than the offense has the ability to block. The offense should be prepared for "hot" throws or sight adjustments.
- Have a variety of launch points for the quarterback. This will help the offense with protections and make the offense less predictable. (The quarterback's launch points are discussed in detail in Chapter 4.)

Aids to Help Protect the Quarterback

Solid Running Game—It is important to have as much balance between run and pass in the offense as possible. The defense should respect the running game.

Mix Up Styles of Protections—Don't limit protections to only one or two types. Defenses are smart and will find a way to get to the quarterback if too few protections are used.

Throw on First Down—Throwing on first down will usually provide your offense with the most basic or predictable defensive coverage to attack.

Utilize Screens/Draws—These plays will slow down an aggressive pass rush.

Keep Down/Distance Reasonable—A good offense should stay out of long yardage situations. Avoid third and long.

Pass Protection Package

A fully developed protection scheme allows a team to be very flexible with its passing game. A functional protection scheme neutralizes the pass rush so that a team has the ability to:

- Throw "hot"
- Flood the field with five receivers out
- Provide maximum protection with only two receivers out
- Provide solid protection to either side of the quarterback
- Use check-down routes with the running backs

Basic dropback protection incorporates a big man rule, in which offensive linemen are assigned to defensive linemen and backs are assigned to linebackers. In this way, there should be neither a size mismatch for the backs, nor a quickness mismatch for the linemen. Also, assigning the backs to linebackers allows them to be incorporated into the pass pattern should their backers drop into coverage.

Types of Protection Schemes

Several basic types of pass protection schemes exist, including dropback, play-action, and sprint out. There are four kinds of dropback pass protection schemes: the quick scheme, the seven-man scheme, the five- and six-man scheme, and the eight-man scheme.

Quick Scheme

This type of dropback pass protection scheme—which includes a three-step drop by the quarterback—is an aggressive scheme that utilizes man/zone principles. In this scheme, the offensive linemen should attack the pass rushes low and hard to create a passing lane for the quarterback. Other three-step protections include slide and wedge schemes.

The quick scheme is an aggressive seven-man protection. The line and H should hold their blocks at the line of scrimmage. The quarterback takes a three-step drop and the ball is gone. The tight end (Y) and H stay in to block. The center will "Rip" or "Liz" to the shade side. The H checks the W linebacker aggressively.

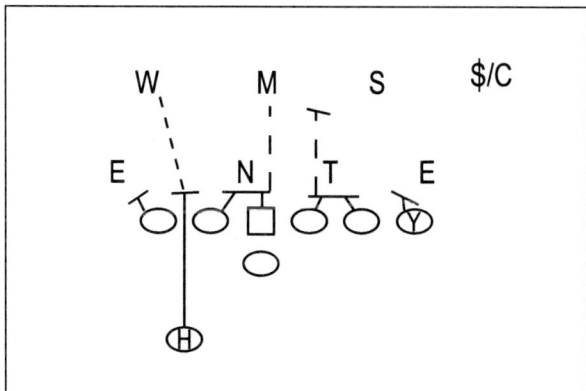

Diagram 5-1. Quick protection (three-step drop)

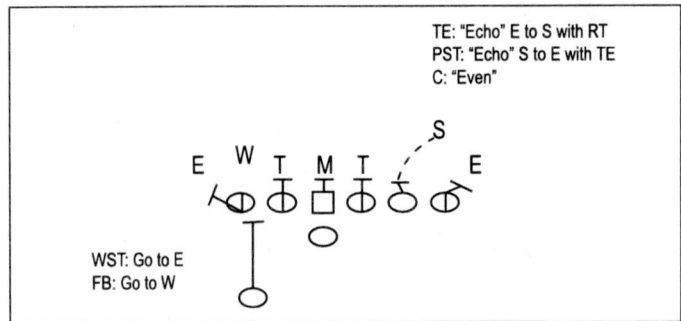

Diagram 5-2. Quick protection versus double eagle

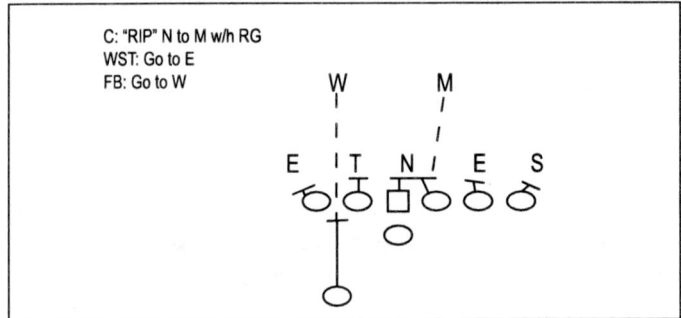

Diagram 5-3. Quick protection versus eagle

Seven-Man Scheme

This type of dropback pass protection scheme—which includes a five- to seven-step drop by the quarterback—involves a group of three different protection schemes (split back, weak flow, or single back). A seven-step scheme is utilized with deep progression reads.

The single-back dropback pass protection scheme can block up to seven rushers. The H will check release 1-2 on the weak side. The center and guards are responsible for the linebackers in the tackle box. They will use a "Rip" or "Liz" call to identify their linebacker. Y will release outside, or stay in and block any edge pressure.

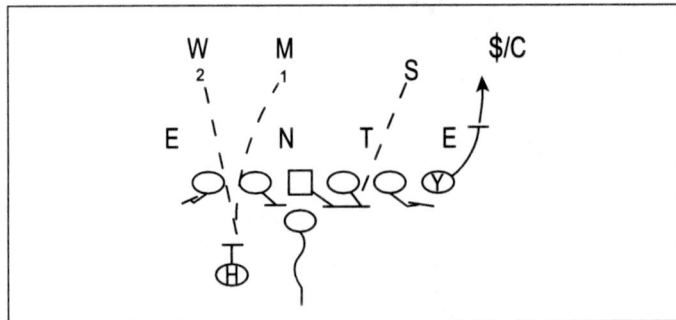

Diagram 5-4. Seven-man protection (single back)

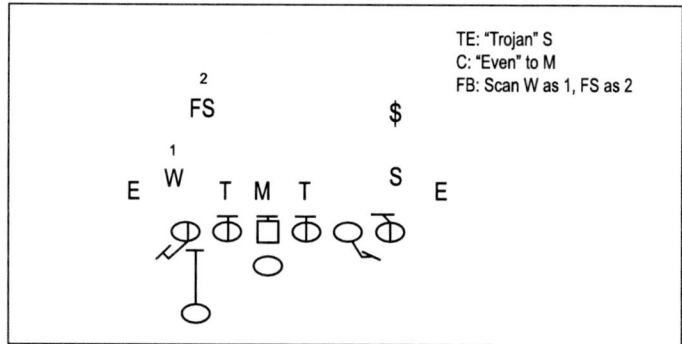

Diagram 5-5. Seven-man protection (single back) versus double eagle

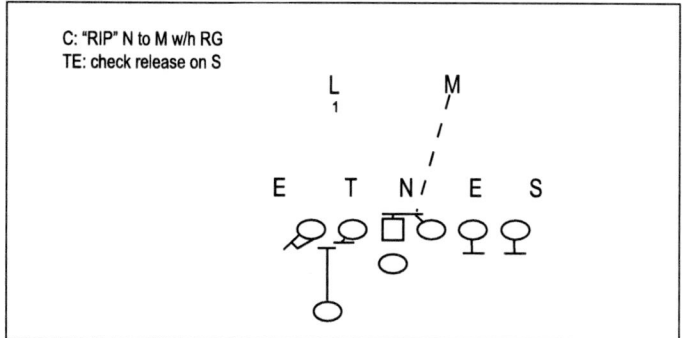

Diagram 5-6. Seven-man protection (single back) versus eagle

The split-back dropback protection can block up to seven rushers. The fullback will check release off the near linebacker. The H will check release the near linebacker to the outside. Y releases outside, and runs through any blitzer. The center will make all "Rip" or "Liz" calls to the Y side.

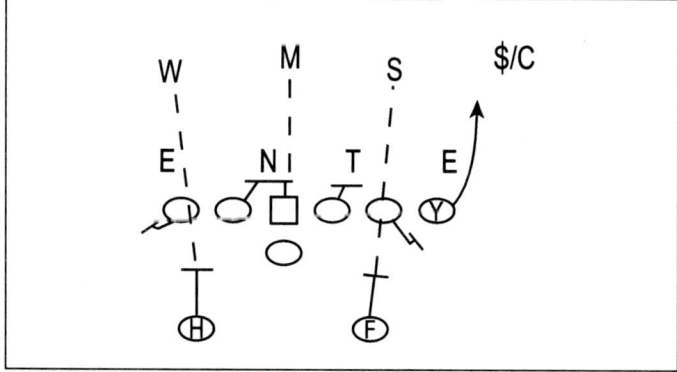

Diagram 5-7. Seven-man protection (split back)

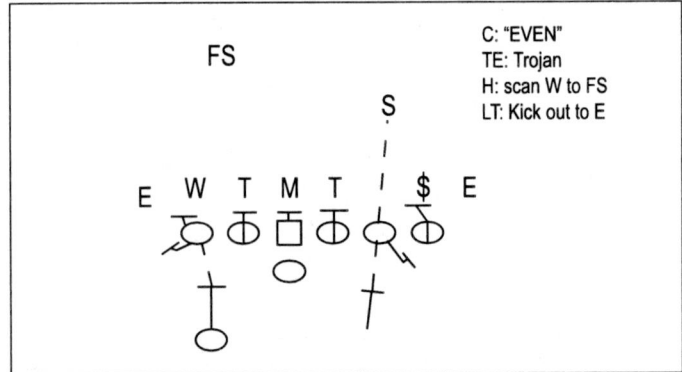

Diagram 5-8. Seven-man protection (split back) versus double eagle

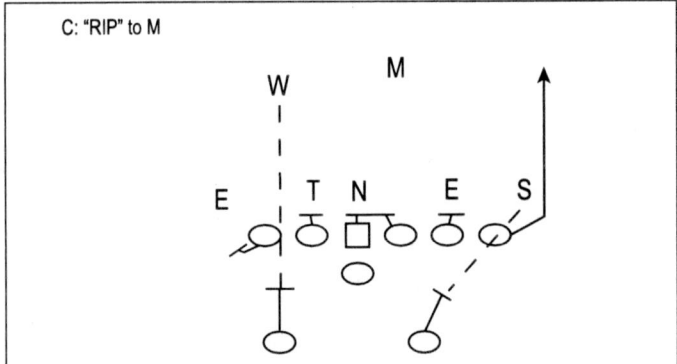

Diagram 5-9. Seven-man protection (split back) versus eagle

Five- and Six-Man Scheme

This type of dropback pass protection scheme requires the quarterback to be responsible for the extra defender (sixth or seventh man), along with the "hot" receiver. It is helpful to use a spread formation when utilizing these protections. This will allow the quarterback and receivers to get a pre-snap look at the defensive alignment.

Six-Man (Single Back) Protection

The single-back dropback pass protection can block up to six rushers. The halfback will scan 1-2 toward Y. Y releases outside and is hot if M and S/S blitz. Note: The center is blocking left (Liz).

The six-man protection scheme has the ability to block six defenders. When the defense brings an *extra* defender, the offense (quarterback and designated receiver) must be prepared for the hot route or sight adjustment. The example in Diagram 5-10b has Z as the hot receiver. The six-man protection scheme versus various defensive fronts is shown in Diagram 5-10c.

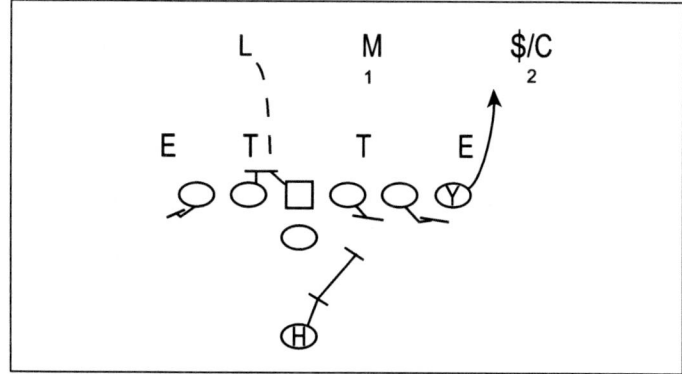

Diagram 5-10a. Six-man protection (single back)

Assignments

Quarterback: 5-step drop (also gun). Hot principle: Z (or drag receiver).

Flanker (Z): Execute drag route. Hot. Zone: Throttle four to six yards. Man coverage: Quick move for rub—be alert to sight adjust.

Split End (X): Run a take-off route (stay wide).

Tight End (Y): Run a take-off route.

Third WR (F): Align 2 to 3 yards from Z. Run a wrap route (12 to 14 yards). Man coverage: Throttle for definite rub.

Halfback (H): Check 63 protection. Run a swing route (if assignment drops into coverage).

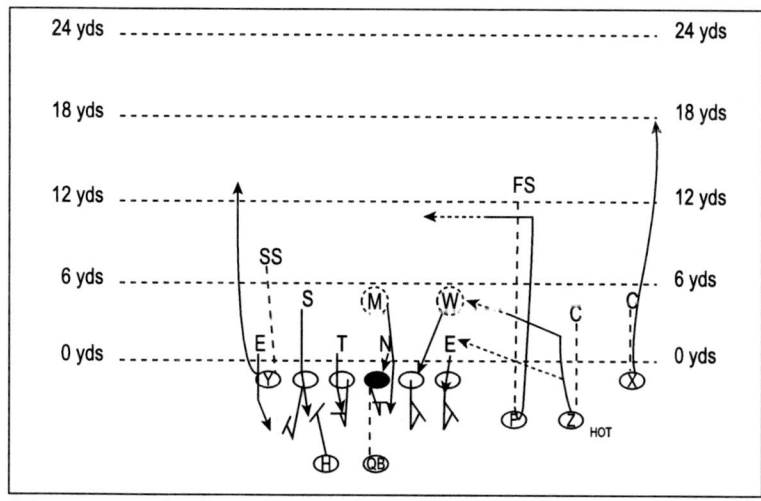

Diagram 5-10b. Six-man protection scheme with Z as the hot receiver

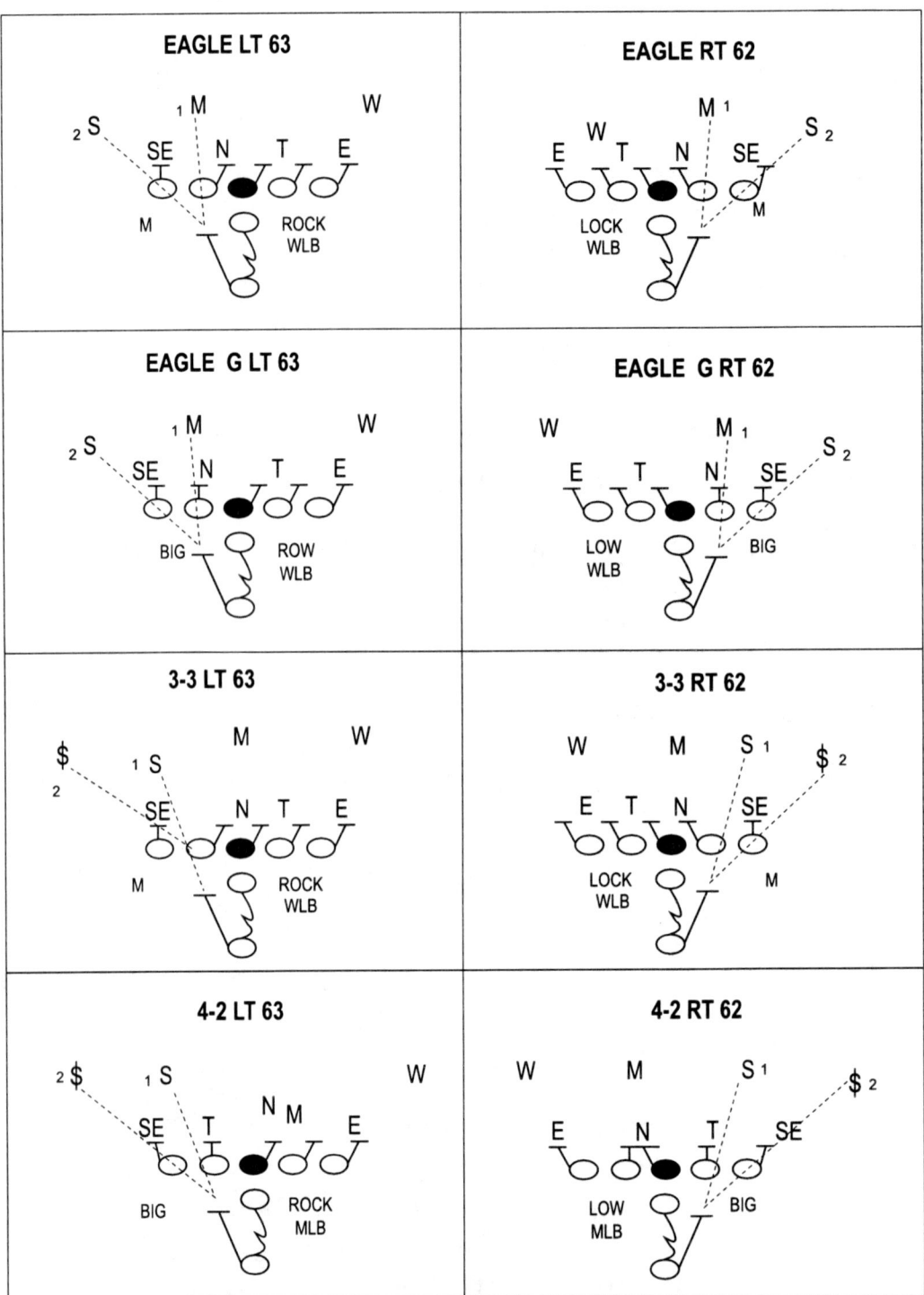

Diagram 5-10c. Six-man protection scheme versus various defensive fronts

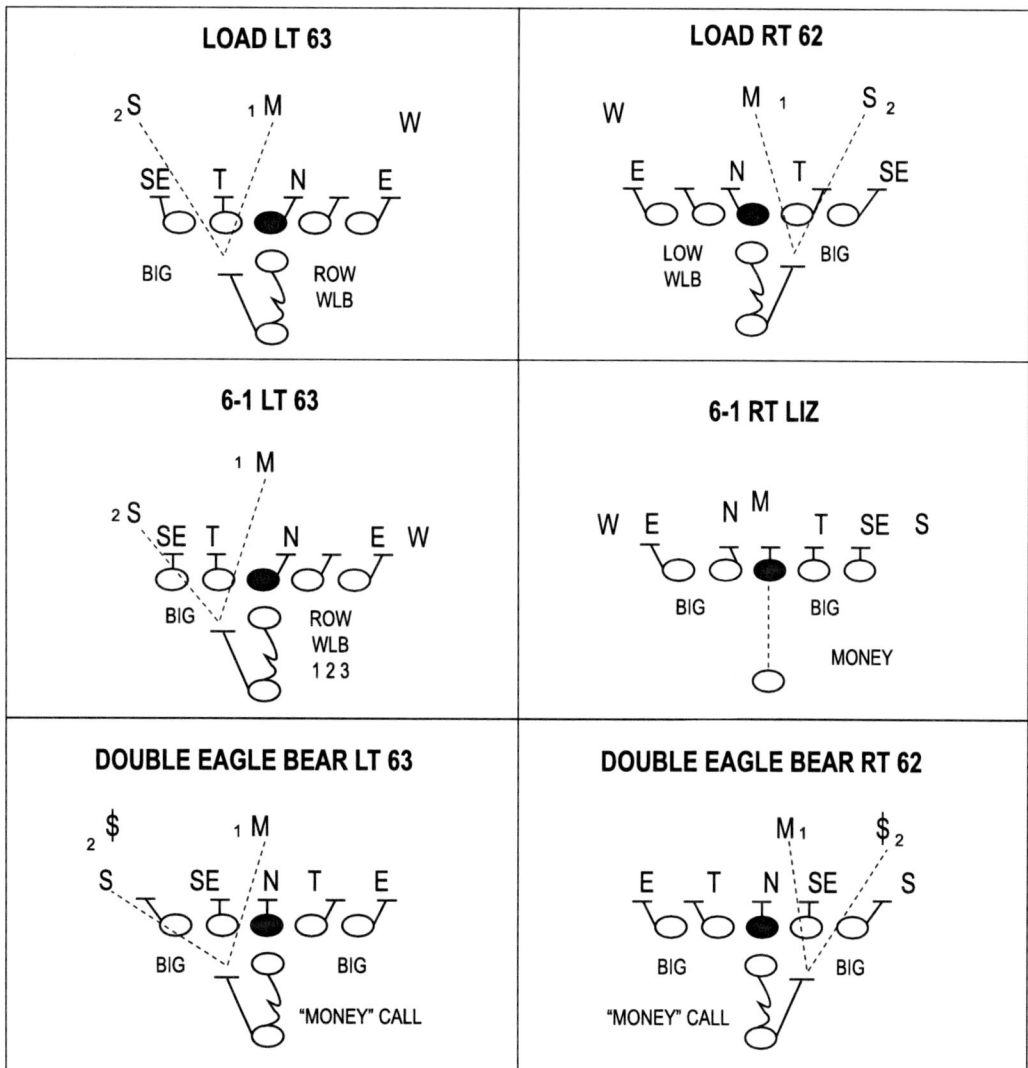

Diagram 5-10c. cont'd.

Five-Man (Empty Backfield) Protection

The empty backfield protection can only block five defenders. In this example, the quarterback and F are responsible for the sixth defender (Will linebacker), with a "hot" throw when he dogs. Note: The center is blocking left (Liz).

The empty backfield protection has the ability to block five defenders. When the defense brings an *extra* defender, the offense (quarterback and designated receiver) must be prepared for the hot route or sight adjustment. The example in Diagram 5-11b has two choices for hot throws (Y and H). The five-man protection versus various defensive fronts is shown in Diagram 5-11c.

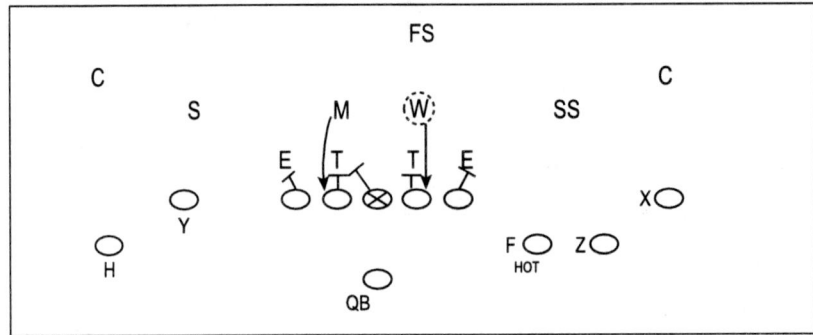

Diagram 5-11a. Five-man protection (empty)

Assignments

Quarterback: 5-step drop (use Gun). Hot principle: H or Y.

Flanker (Z): Run a choice route (eight yards).

Split End (X): Run a curl route (14 yards)—no conversion.

Tight End (Y): Inside release. Run a scat route (eight yards). Possible sight adjustment: inside linebacker. Zone coverage: find the hole. Man coverage: accelerate outside. Hot: Sam/Mike linebacker.

Third WR (F): Run a take-off route. Release outside (stay wide).

Halfback (H): Run a scat route. Look quick for the ball (hot). Adjust alignment to tackle/tight end gap.

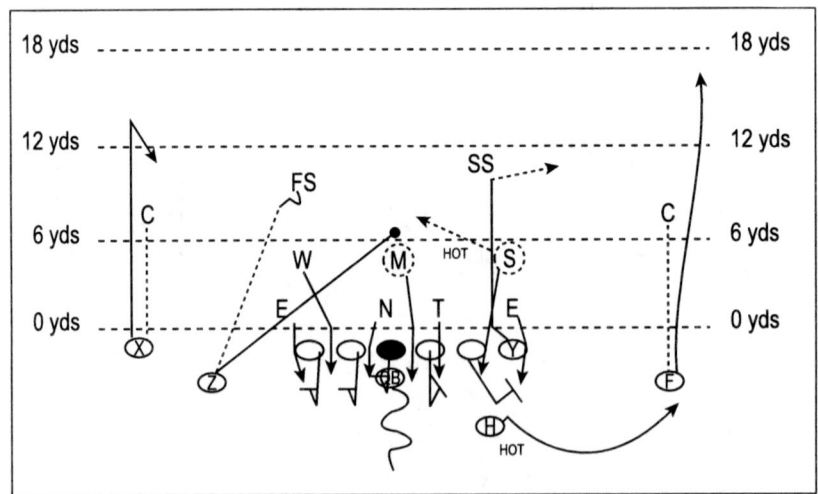

Diagram 5-11b. Five-man protection with Y and H as hot receivers

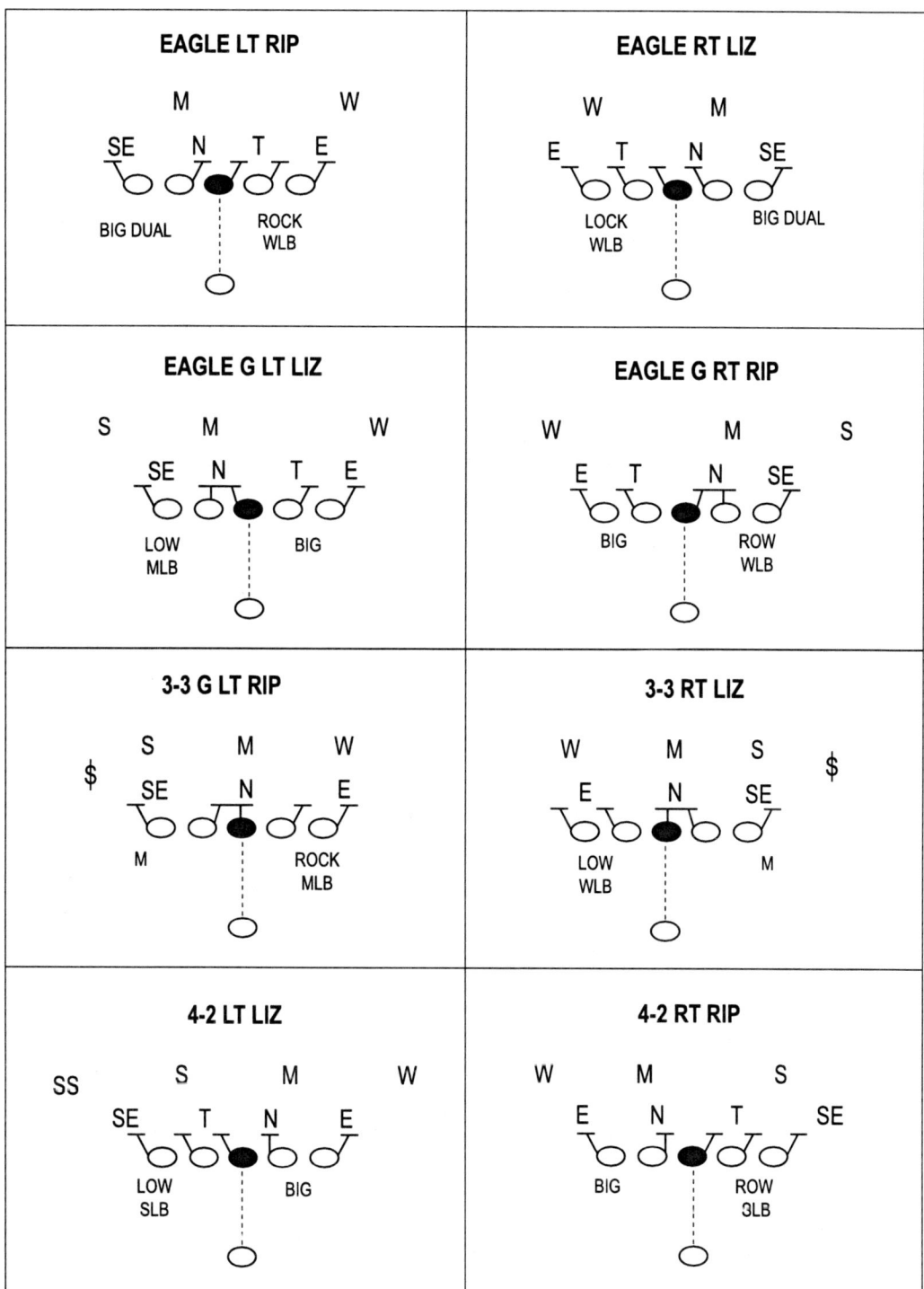

Diagram 5-11c. Five-man protection versus various defensive fronts

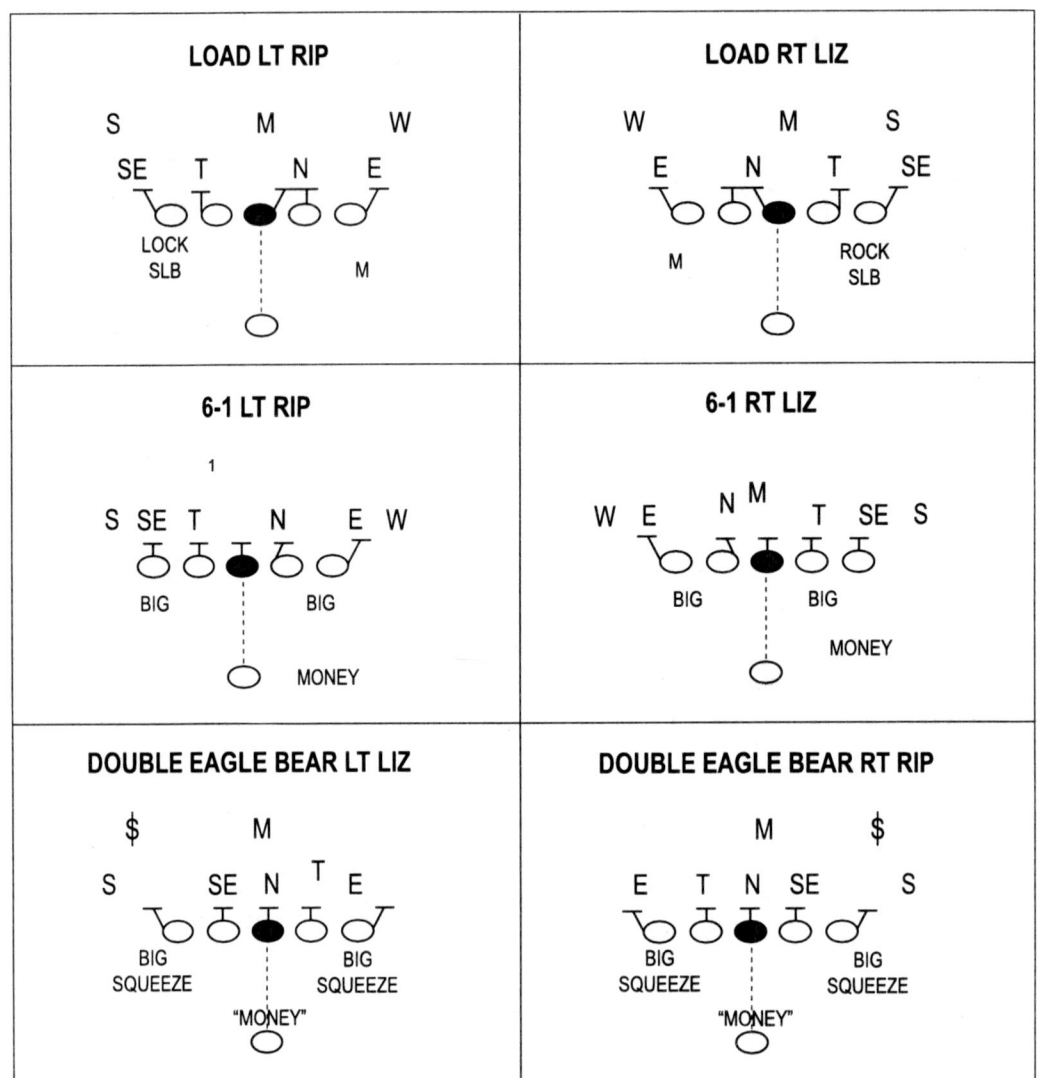

Diagram 5-11c. cont'd.

Eight-Man Scheme

This type of dropback pass protection keeps the running backs and the tight end in to block. An eight-man protection scheme is used predominantly in a team's audible package to pick up an eight-man blitz (max protection). Although the eight-man scheme limits the number of receivers in the pattern to two, if properly executed it will give both wide receivers an opportunity to go deep by enabling them to break off their second cut.

Other Basic Protections

Play-Action Passes—Complements the core running game, including boots and nakeds.

Sprint-Out Passes—Complements a mobile quarterback with pass/run threat. This is an excellent scheme versus a defense that gives a lot of pass rush pressure up the middle.

Dash—Complements an offense that utilizes the gun alignment. It gives the offense an organized moving pocket from the gun.

Basic Offensive Line Fundamentals and Techniques—The Stance

The starting position for any football play is the stance. The stance must be fundamentally sound to execute offensive line techniques consistently. Most offensive linemen have two stances—a two-point stance and a three-point stance. The two-point is primarily for pass situations and the three-point is primarily for run situations. It is important to be able to run or pass out of either stance.

Linemen should learn both a right-handed and left-handed stance. The feet should be shoulder-width apart or slightly wider. If a player is to the right of the center, then the toe of his right foot should be set back to the heel or middle of his left foot. The opposite is true for a player to the left of the center. The reason for this is to provide power and stability to the inside, and quick reaction to the outside versus a speed rush by a defensive lineman. This also provides a natural stagger in the feet, giving the player better balance when pulled forward or pushed backward. The center's feet remain square in a side-by-side position in the stance. Once the ball is snapped, he staggers his feet.

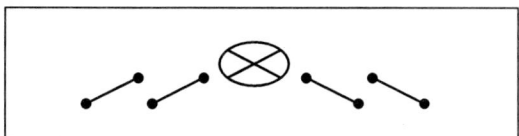

Diagram 5-12. Toe-heel foot placement

In the two-point stance, there should be 45-degree angles at the foot and ankle, the ankle and thigh, and the thigh and hip. These are power angles. The hands should rest lightly above the knee, ready to fire up and out onto the defender. The weight is over the balls of the feet with a tiny bit of daylight under the heel of the outside foot.

Diagram 5-13. Two-point stance

The three-point stance is similar to the two-point. There are power angles at the foot and ankle and at the ankle and thigh. The outside hand is placed on the ground. The weight is on the balls of the feet, not the hand. The lineman should be able to move the hand easily.

Diagram 5-14. Three-point stance

Footwork Drills

Jumping Ropes

Objective: To develop foot speed, reaction, and coordination

Description: Do each style of jump for 40 seconds. Rest for 30 seconds between each style.

Straight jump—Jump the rope with both feet at the same time with the rope coming forward.

Backward—Jump the rope with both feet at the same time with the rope going backward.

Side-to-side—Jump the rope with both feet, jumping side-to-side in a slalom motion.

Run in place—Jump the rope while moving the feet in a running motion.

Shuffle—Jump the rope while moving each foot forward and backward in a shuffle motion.

Jacks—Jump the rope while moving the feet in a jumping jack motion.

One foot—Jump the rope with one foot. Jump with each foot three times, then switch to the other foot.

Crossovers—Jump the rope while crossing the right foot over the left, then crossing the left foot over the right.

Rocking—Set the right foot forward and the left foot back. Jump the rope while rocking forward on the right foot and backward on the left. Midway through the allotted time, the coach will yell, "Switch." When this happens, put the left foot forward and the right foot back and continue.

Running Ropes

Objective: To develop foot speed, reaction, and coordination

Description: The whole group of linemen goes through the ropes forward and backward during each exercise. The linemen should keep both hands extended and the elbows locked in a pass protection position. The hips should be low, in good football position. Emphasize technique over speed.

Every box—The right foot hits every box on the right side and the left foot hits every box on the left side. The order that the steps are taken is indicated by the number.

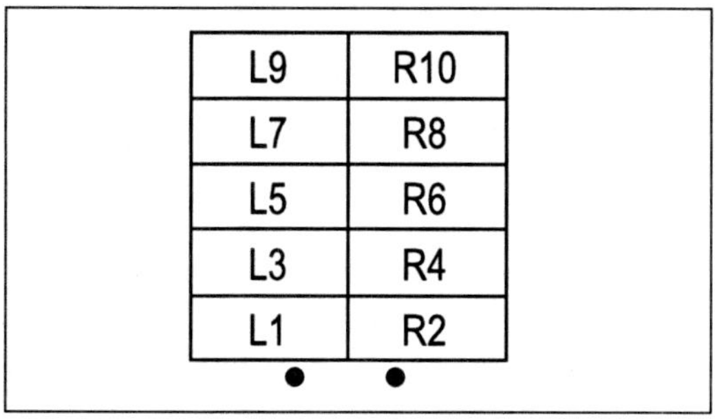

L9	R10
L7	R8
L5	R6
L3	R4
L1	R2

Diagram 5-15. Every box drill

Every other box—The right foot hits every other box on the right side, as does the left foot on the left side.

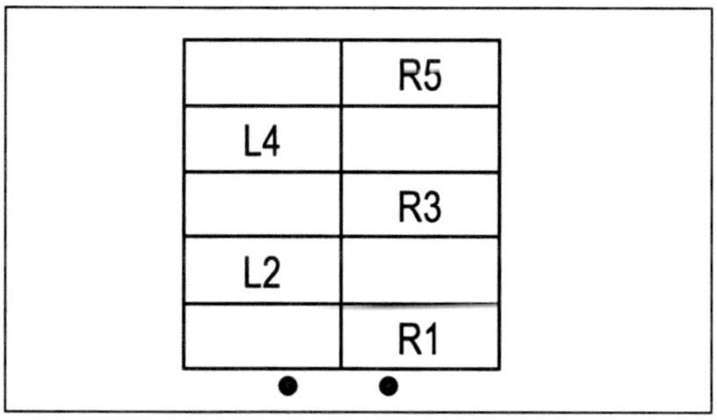

	R5
L4	
	R3
L2	
	R1

Diagram 5-16. Every other box drill

Zig-zag—The player goes through the ropes in the manner shown in Diagram 5-17.

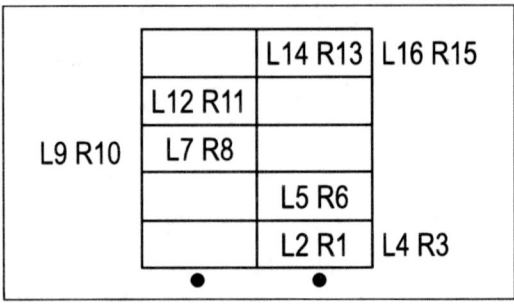

Diagram 5-17. Zig-zag drill

Typewriter (forward and backward)—The player moves the feet across the ropes like the carriage of a typewriter. Have players do repetitions of this drill facing forward and backward.

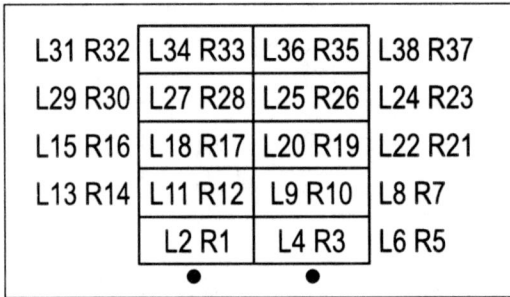

Diagram 5-18. Typewriter drill

Sideways—This is similar to the typewriter, but the player goes the length of the ropes. Have the players perform repetitions going toward the right and the left.

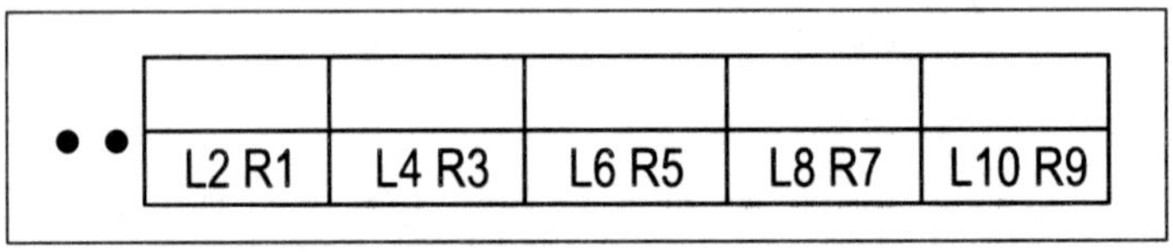

Diagram 5-19. Sideways drill

Three steps each box—the player steps into the box one foot at a time, and then takes three quick steps in place before moving on to the next box. This is repeated in each box.

Hip Drills

Softball Roll

Objective: For the player to keep his hips low and back straight, similar to a shortstop fielding a ground ball

Description: The player and coach stand facing each other about five to 10 yards apart. The coach rolls the ball to the right, left, or directly at the player. The player fields the ball between his legs by moving his feet. To field the ball, the player squats with his hips low, back straight, and shoulders square to the coach. He tosses the ball back to the coach and this is repeated several times. The emphasis is on body position, not the ability to field grounders.

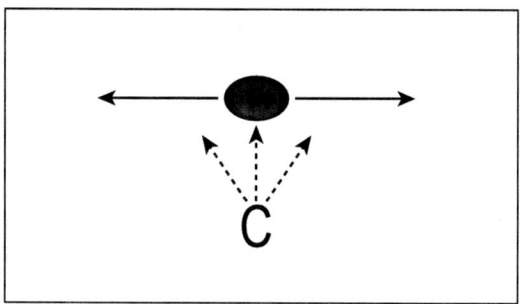

Diagram 5-20. Softball roll drill

Duck Walk Stride

Objective: To teach the linemen to keep their hips low and to move fluidly from a power-type position

Description: The player exaggerates a long, low stride, with hips low and the back straight. This movement should be performed slowly and deliberately, but with a fluid motion. Have each player do this several times, going 10 yards each time.

Diagram 5-21. Duck walk stride drill

Duck Walk Stomp

Objective: To keep the hips low and work the feet solidly against the ground

Description: The player walks in an exaggerated stomping motion, with the hips low. Each player does several sets of 10 yards each. A variation of this is having all the players follow the leader and work the duck walk forward, backward, and to either side.

Walk Back with Resistance

Objective: To keep the hips low and to keep the feet solid when pass protecting. This drill also teaches the linemen to lose a little ground at a time to maintain good body position.

Description: The offensive player puts both hands behind his back with his body in a good position to pass protect. The defensive player pushes the offensive player and forces him back. The offensive player works to lose as little ground as possible, while also staying square and in a good position with the defensive player. The offensive player needs to resist without leaning forward. The defensive player should occasionally try to pull the offensive player forward to see if he can catch him being overextended.

Fit-Walk-Lockout

Objective: To teach the proper fundamentals of run blocking

Description: The player slowly walks through all three elements of run blocking. The lineman fits his facemask in the numbers of the defender and his hands should rest at the bottom of the defender's numbers. The lineman should contact the defender at three points—facemask and both hands. While maintaining this position, the lineman begins the duck walk and forces the defender backward. Once the lineman has control, he should lock out his arms and finish the block. This is done at half speed for good technique.

Fit and Chop

Objective: To teach the proper fundamentals of run blocking

Description: The lineman must fit properly into the defender's numbers. The defender gives resistance and the lineman maintains good position, chops his feet, and moves the defender about 20 yards. As the lineman gets control, he should lock out. This drill is similar to Fit-Walk-Lockout, but is faster and with more resistance.

Offensive Line Pass Protection Drills

The following drills will aid in developing proper individual pass protection techniques.

Set-Up

Objective: To teach set-up and quick punch

Description: The linemen must maintain a good stance while holding a medicine ball. Then, have them set up and throw the ball up and out, reminding them to really snap it out. Also, remind the linemen to focus on having quick feet. Have them perform several repetitions

Coaching Points:
- Have the linemen lift the ball straight up and then out.
- Teach linemen to have a quick punch.
- Remind linemen to keep the hips low.

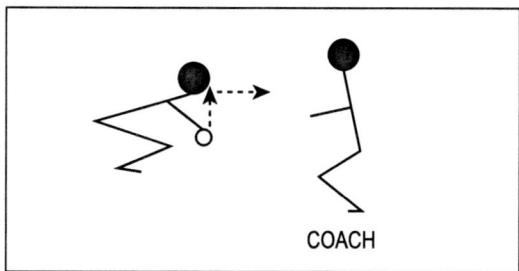

Diagram 5-22. Set-up drill

Quick Set

Objective: To teach the quick set-up

Description: The coach throws the medicine ball toward a lineman. While maintain a good stance, the lineman sets up and punches the ball back at the coach. Remind the lineman to focus on having quick feet. Have each player perform several repetitions.

Coaching Points:
- Remind the players to snap up quickly, use the heels of the hands, and keep the thumbs up and the elbows in.
- Linemen should always focus on keeping the hips low and having quick feet.
- Throw the ball quick and hard.

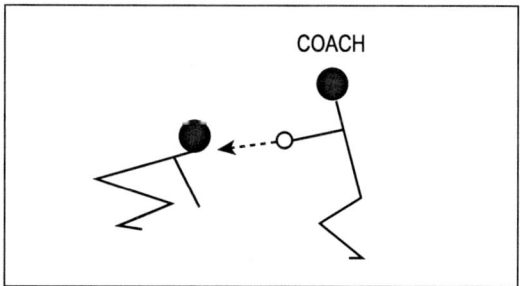

Diagram 5-23. Quick set drill

Catch

Objective: To teach footwork and punch for pass protection

Description: Begin the drill by partnering up the offensive linemen, who will chop the feet down the line while playing catch with a medicine ball. Have them place the proper foot up in the direction of movement, keeping the arms up the entire time. Remind them to really snap the ball out.

Coaching Points:
- Remind the linemen to keep the hips down, have choppy feet, and perform a quick snap.
- The arms should form a slight "V."

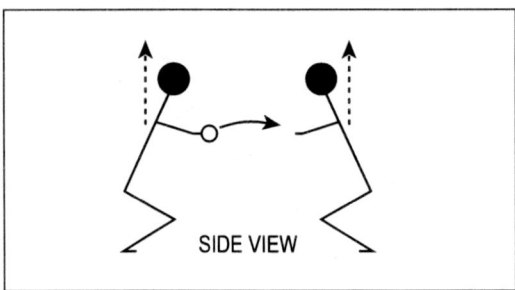

Diagram 5-24. Catch drill

Sets

Objective: To teach set-up for pass protection

Description: Each lineman sets up on command, snaps up, and maintains quick feet until the reset. Repeat this drill several times

Variation: A defender puts his hands on the back of the lineman's head while he is in his stance. Before the snap, the lineman pushes against the hands with his head. On the snap, the defender moves his hands, forcing the lineman to get out of the stance quickly.

Coaching Points:
- This drill should focus on quickness.
- Remind the players to keep the hips low and the head and chest up.
- The players must have quick feet.

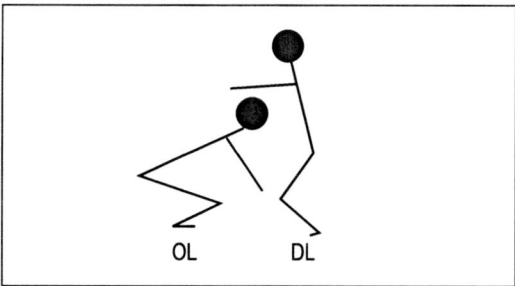

Diagram 5-25. Sets drill

Partner Sets

Objective: To teach set-up and hand placement for pass protection

Description: Have the players set up on command. When the lineman snaps up, the defender should step into the lineman and reach very deliberately. The lineman should then punch his hands inside the defender's numbers and underneath his breast pad. Remind the players to have quick feet until the reset. Repeat this drill several times.

Coaching Points:
- Remind the linemen to keep the hands inside and underneath.
- Have them perform a quick set, keeping the hips low and maintaining quick feet.
- The defender should be lined up almost offside.

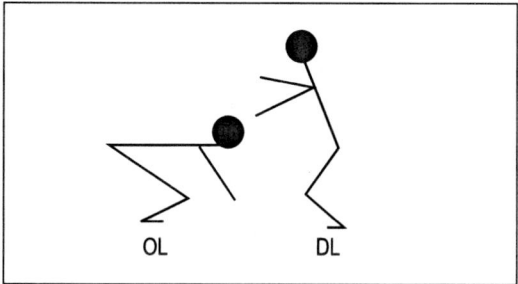

Diagram 5-26. Partner sets drill

Partner Slide

Objective: To teach hand placement and body position for pass protection

Description: Have the linemen partner up. One man walks while the other man chops and punches the shoulders. The players should put the proper foot up in direction of movement.

Coaching Points:
- Remind the players to stay square and low.
- Teach the linemen to keep the thumbs together and punch up and out.
- Players should place the lead foot forward.
- The defender should fall into the lineman, and the lineman should punch him back to an upright position.

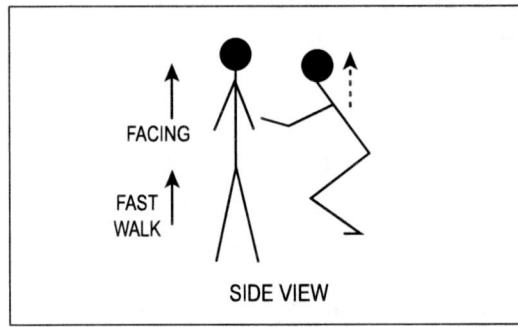

Diagram 5-27. Partner slide drill

Mirror Drill

Objective: To teach the basic principles of pass protection

Description: Place two cones five yards apart on a line. The lineman puts his heels just in front of the line and the defender faces the lineman. When the drill begins, the defender tries to cross the line. When the defender is able to cross the line, he scores one point. The defender should try to score as many points as possible in a 10- to 15-second period. The defender should only use speed-type moves (e.g., swim, spin, head fakes), but no bull-rush. After one man goes on offense, he should then go on defense.

Coaching Points:
- Remind the players to stay square and low.
- Teach the linemen to keep the thumbs together and punch up and out.
- Players should place the lead foot forward.
- The defender should fall into the lineman, and the lineman should punch him back to an upright position.

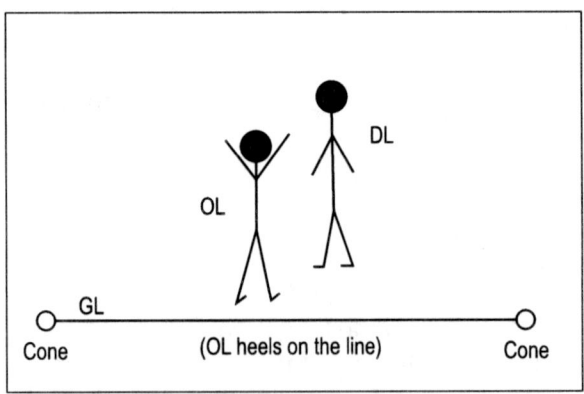

Diagram 5-28. Mirror drill

6

Innovative Practice and Game Planning

A lot of time should be spent in meetings, studying video, executing drills, and then viewing practice video. A good coach leaves no stone unturned. Game planning is an ongoing process throughout the week. All situations should be covered, including goal line/short yardage, red zone, two-point plays, and the two-minute offense.

The coordinator/play caller should work on the game day play-call form throughout the week, making minor adjustments after each practice. All decisions should be made at least 24 hours before the game. A good offensive coordinator will have played the game in his mind many times before the team steps on the field. He must study his opponent and know how it will react in certain situations, leaving no chance for surprises.

It is a good practice to script the first 10 plays and emphasize different personnel groupings, formations, motions, and shifts so the coach can see how the defense reacts. The offense should run the scripted plays in a walk-through practice the day before the game. This lets the players know what to expect, helps the offense be confident of their assignments, and guarantees that the ball will be in the playmakers' hands.

It is very important to organize practices and establish game plans that cover all elements of the game. Practice and game plans will reflect directly on a team's success. How a team prepares has a correlation to how the team will play.

> "Don't mistake activity for achievement. Practice it the right way."
> –John Wooden
> Hall-of-Fame Basketball Coach
> UCLA

> "Practice without improvement is meaningless."
> –Chuck Knox
> Former Head Football Coach
> Seattle Seahawks

The forms in this chapter will aid in practice preparation and in developing measurable feedback for the coaches and players to interpret. The quarterback and wide receiver drill checklists in Diagrams 6-1 and 6-2 help each position coach plan his "individual" practice time and ensure that all necessary fundamentals and

QUARTERBACK DRILL CHECKLIST

DRILL	DATES									
Stance										
C/Q exchange (reg)										
C/Q exchange (gun)										
Quick feet										
One-knee throws										
Two-knee throws										
Sideways throws										
Circle throws										
Spot throws										
Wave drill										
Flush drill										
Tracks										
Faking										
3-step drop										
5-step drop										
7-step drop										
Gun drops										
Dash										
Nakeds										
Sprint out										
Boots										
Cadence										
Audibles										
Hand signals										

Diagram 6-1. Quarterback practice progression checklist

WIDE RECEIVER DRILL CHECKLIST

CATCHING	DATES								
Woofle ball									
Warm-up									
Perimeter									
Pat-n-go									
Turn ("Ball")									
Turn & go									
Pole									
Pro-pal									
Blaster									
Blurr									
Last phase of curl									
Sideline									
Tightrope									
Highest point									
Defender									
Jug (reg. & close)									
Dive									
Fingertip drills									
RELEASES									
Big bag (space)									
Extra DB's									
Cover 2									
Throw by									
ROUTES									
Top of routes									
Routes vs. Air									
M/M									
BREAK POINT									
Square									
Zag									
In/Out									
3-step									
Y.A.C.									
Score									
BALL SECURITY									
"See" tuck									
Strip									
Gauntlet									
BLOCKING									
Stalk									
Cut									
Crack									
Force recog.									
Sled									
Mirror									

Diagram 6-2. Wide receiver practice progression checklist

techniques will be practiced. A variety of drills should be used in practice while developing specific skills for the position.

The offensive practice plan shown in Diagram 6-3 should be completed by the offensive staff prior to each practice session. This will aid in overall organization and accountability.

OFFENSIVE PRACTICE PLAN

Type of Practice _____ Date _____

TIME	PERIOD	O-LINE	TIGHT ENDS	BACKS	WR'S	QB'S

REMINDERS: INSERTION: INDIVIDUAL DRILLS:

Diagram 6-3. Basic offensive practice plan

The practice script of plays shown in Diagram 6-4 includes the following information:
- Drill—Inside run, pass skeleton, team, etc.
- Situation—First down, third down, red zone, goal line, etc.
- Position—Left hash, middle, right hash. It is important to move the ball to various hashes and yard lines so the players will understand field location.
- Scripted plays—Include personnel grouping, formation/motion, play, and defensive front/coverage.

```
                          PRACTICE SCRIPT
                                              Date _____

       DRILL: _____        SITUATION: _____

       POSITION: LEFT                  POSITION: RIGHT
       1. _____              1. _____
       2. _____              2. _____
       3. _____              3. _____
       4. _____              4. _____
       5. _____              5. _____
       6. _____              6. _____
       7. _____              7. _____
       8. _____              8. _____
       9. _____              9. _____
       10. _____              10. _____
       11. _____              11. _____
       12. _____              12. _____
       13. _____              13. _____
       14. _____              14. _____
       15. _____              15. _____

                          POSITION: MIDDLE
                          1. _____
                          2. _____
                          3. _____
                          4. _____
                          5. _____
                          6. _____
```

Diagram 6-4. Practice script of plays by hash

The chart in Diagram 6-5 helps keep a record of the number of times a particular play is practiced during either a single practice session or during the week, or executed in a game.

An explosive offense makes the opponent defend the complete field. The chart in Diagram 6-6 will act as a visual aid to ensure that the offense is attacking all areas. It can be used during practice or during games as a method to self-scout.

The pass skelly/scrimmage results chart in Diagram 6-7 can be completed either during practice or at the conclusion of practice to supply a thorough summary of each play.
- Play—Personnel grouping, formation, play called
- Quarterback—Jersey number of quarterback involved
- Time—Release time of each throw (from snap to release)
- Coverage—List coverage by defense

PLAY FREQUENCY CHART

Opponent _____ Date _____

FORMATION (PERSONNEL)	PLAY	#	DIRECTIONAL BREAKDOWN	COMMENTS

Diagram 6-5. Play frequency chart

- X, Y, Z, F, H—List the receiver thrown to in proper column by jersey number
- Completion—Mark if a completion resulted
- Incompletion—Mark if an incompletion resulted
- Comments—Other possibilities (interception, sack, hurry, dropped pass, etc.)

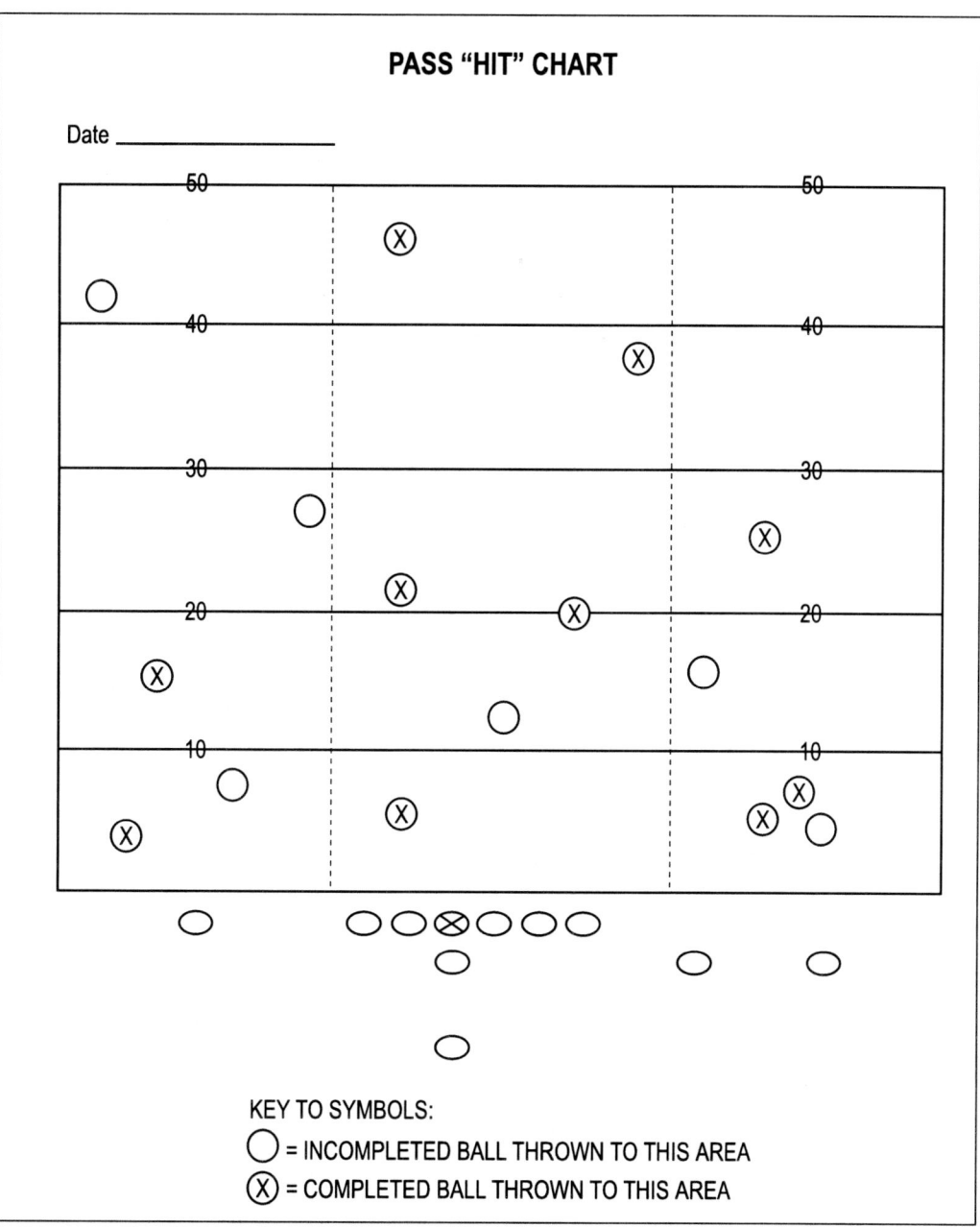

Diagram 6-6. Pass "hit" chart

The passing totals (scrimmage/skeleton) chart in Diagram 6-8 is a valuable tool in summarizing offensive skilled personnel performance in the passing game. Cumulative results of each player's production are recorded during spring practice and again during the fall preseason.

NO	PLAY	QB	TIME	COV	X	Y	Z	F	H	COMP	INC	COMMENTS
1												
2												
3												
4												
5												
6												
7												
8												
9												
10												
11												
12												
13												
14												
15												
16												
17												
18												
19												
20												

PASS SKELLY/SCRIMMAGE RESULTS

Date _____

Diagram 6-7. Pass skelly/scrimmage results chart

The "move the ball versus scout team" script in Diagram 6-9 should be completed with plays/situations from that week's game plan. This mini-script is used to organize the short practice on the day prior to the game to review all crucial offensive situations.

PASSING TOTALS (SCRIMMAGE/SKELETON)

ATT: _____ COMP: _____ DROP: _____ FLUSH: _____ INT: _____ PCT: _____

QB	ATT	COMP/PCT	INT	DROPS	FLUSH	SACKS

TE'S	CATCHES	DROPS	PCT.

WR'S	CATCHES	DROPS	PCT.

RB'S	CATCHES	DROPS	PCT.

SUMMARY	CATCHES	DROPS	PCT.

Diagram 6-8. Passing totals chart

MOVE THE BALL vs. SCOUT

-4 COMING OUT

1. _____   1. _____

-30 YL (Field Plays)

1. _____   1. _____
2. _____   2. _____

                1. _____

+50 YL (Special Plays)

1. _____
2. _____
3. _____
4. _____
5. _____

+20 YL (Blitz/Red Zone)

1. _____   1. _____
2. _____   2. _____

                1. _____
                2. _____

+4 YL (Goal Line)

1. _____   1. _____
2. _____   2. _____

Two Pt. Plays: 1. _____
                      2. _____

Review: Milk the Clock   Save the Game   Victory O.T.L   Clock   Kill
              Sideline Huddle   Time Outs   25 Second Clock   Substitutions

Diagram 6-9. Move the ball versus scout team script

The two game day charts shown in Diagram 6-10 are indispensable for press box/sideline organization. The charts will list the best possible plays to attack the opponent's defensive tendencies.

SAMPLE GAME PLAN

Game Plan vs. _____   Date _____

SCRIPT

1. _____
2. _____
3. _____
4. _____
5. _____
6. _____
7. _____
8. _____
9. _____
10. _____

3rd & 7
1. _____
2. _____
3. _____
4. _____
5. _____

GOAL LINE

| FRONTS | BLITZ | COV. |
| RUN | | PASS |

RUN
1. _____
2. _____
3. _____
4. _____
5. _____

PASS
1. _____
2. _____
3. _____
4. _____
5. _____

INCHES 1. _____
4th INCHES 1. _____

NORMAL DOWNS

RUNS

ONE BACK
1. _____
2. _____
3. _____
4. _____
5. _____
6. _____
7. _____
8. _____

TWO BACK
1. _____
2. _____
3. _____
4. _____
5. _____
6. _____
7. _____
8. _____

MOVEMENT PASSES

P.A.P
1. _____
2. _____
3. _____
4. _____
5. _____
6. _____
7. _____
8. _____

SPRINT
1. _____
2. _____
3. _____
4. _____
5. _____
6. _____
7. _____
8. _____

3 STEP
1. _____
2. _____
3. _____
4. _____
5. _____

5 STEP (CONTROL)
1. _____
2. _____
3. _____
4. _____
5. _____
6. _____
7. _____
8. _____
9. _____
10. _____

SCREENS
1. _____
2. _____
3. _____
4. _____
5. _____

THIRD DOWN

3rd 1-2

FRONT BLITZ COV.

RUNS
1. _____
2. _____
3. _____
4. _____
5. _____

PASS
1. _____
2. _____
3. _____
4. _____
5. _____

3rd 3-6

FRONT BLITZ COV.

RUN
1. _____
2. _____
3. _____
4. _____
5. _____

PASSES
1. _____
2. _____
3. _____
4. _____
5. _____

PAP/MOVT.
1. _____
2. _____
3. _____
4. _____
5. _____

SCREENS/SPECIALS
1. _____
2. _____
3. _____
4. _____
5. _____

3rd 7-10

FRONT BLITZ COV.

RUN
1. _____
2. _____
3. _____
4. _____
5. _____

MOVT.
1. _____
2. _____
3. _____
4. _____
5. _____

PASSES
1. _____
2. _____
3. _____
4. _____
5. _____

SCREENS/SPECIALS
1. _____
2. _____
3. _____
4. _____
5. _____

Diagram 6-10. Game plan

Game Plan vs. _____

RED ZONE

+20 YL
FRONT   BLITZ   COV.

RUN
1. _____
2. _____
3. _____
4. _____
5. _____

PASS
1. _____
2. _____
3. _____
4. _____
5. _____

P.A.P./SPRINT
1. _____
2. _____
3. _____
4. _____
5. _____

SCREEN/SPECIALS
1. _____
2. _____
3. _____
4. _____
5. _____

+10 YL
FRONT   BLITZ   COV.

RUN
1. _____
2. _____
3. _____
4. _____
5. _____

PASSES
1. _____
2. _____
3. _____
4. _____
5. _____

P.A.P./SPRINT
1. _____
2. _____
3. _____
4. _____
5. _____

SPECIALS
1. _____
2. _____
3. _____
4. _____
5. _____

COMING OUT
FRONT   BLITZ   COV.

RUN
1. _____
2. _____
3. _____
4. _____

PASS
1. _____
2. _____
3. _____
4. _____

GADGETS
1. _____
2. _____
3. _____
4. _____
5. _____

MILK CLOCK

RUN
1. _____
2. _____
3. _____
4. _____

PASS
1. _____
2. _____
3. _____
4. _____

TWO POINT PLAYS
1. _____
2. _____

VICTORY OFFENSE
1. _____
2. _____

CRITICAL SITUATIONS

LAST PLAY
1. _____
2. _____
3. _____
4. _____

25 SECONDS 1st & 10
1. _____
2. _____
3. _____
4. _____

TWO MINUTE OFFENSE: READY LIST

RUNS

PASSES

NOTES:

HOME RUNS
1. _____
2. _____
3. _____
4. _____

Diagram 6-10. cont'd.

The chart in Diagram 6-11 is used to script plays in between offensive series while the defense is on the field. It serves as a worksheet to organize the play selection for the next series on offense.

The offensive breakdown chart in Diagram 6-12 is completed during video or in-person scouting of the opponent, or on game day (usually from the press box).

GAME NEW SERIES

SERIES
1. __________
2. __________
3. __________
4. __________
5. __________

SERIES
1. __________
2. __________
3. __________
4. __________
5. __________

SERIES
1. __________
2. __________
3. __________
4. __________
5. __________

SERIES
1. __________
2. __________
3. __________
4. __________
5. __________

SERIES
1. __________
2. __________
3. __________
4. __________
5. __________

SERIES
1. __________
2. __________
3. __________
4. __________
5. __________

ATTACK MODE
1. __________
2. __________
3. __________
4. __________
5. __________

SETTLE DOWN
1. __________
2. __________
3. __________
4. __________
5. __________

Diagram 6-11. Game: New series chart

OFFENSE BREAKDOWN FORM

Opponent: _______________ Page: __________

PLY#	FIELD POSITION	HASH	DOWN	DIST.	PLAY/ FORMATION	FRONT	SLANT	DOGS	BLITZ	COV.	COMMENTS	TIME CODE

Diagram 6-12. Offensive breakdown chart

The defensive summary chart in Diagram 6-13 is used to record the defenses' tendencies by down/distance and hash mark during the game. Write the front/coverage in the approximate space to visualize the defensive plan of attack.

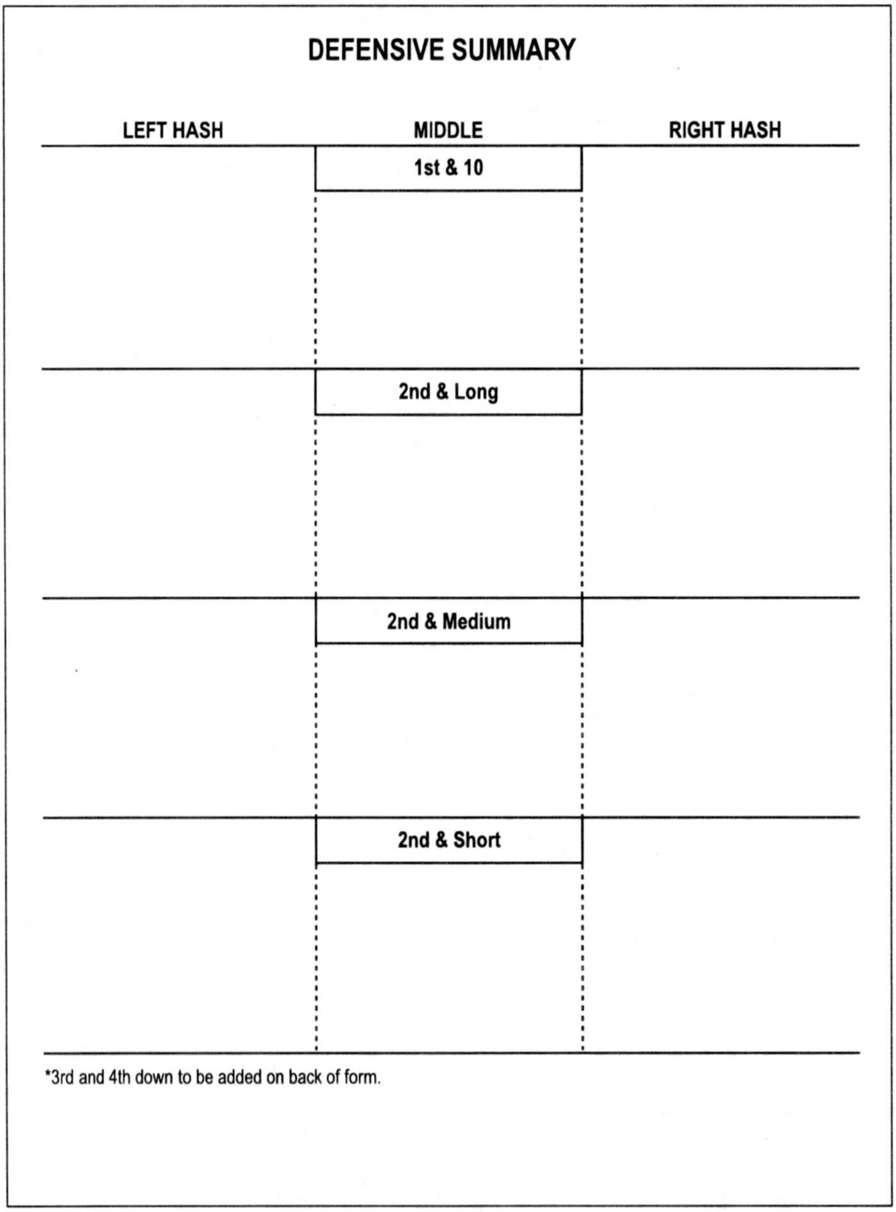

DEFENSIVE SUMMARY

LEFT HASH	MIDDLE	RIGHT HASH
	1st & 10	
	2nd & Long	
	2nd & Medium	
	2nd & Short	

*3rd and 4th down to be added on back of form.

Diagram 6-13. Defensive summary chart

The game summary by formation chart in Diagram 6-14 is used to record the defenses' tendencies by formation and strength call. It should be reviewed after each series, quarter, and at halftime to counter defensive tendencies and adjustments.

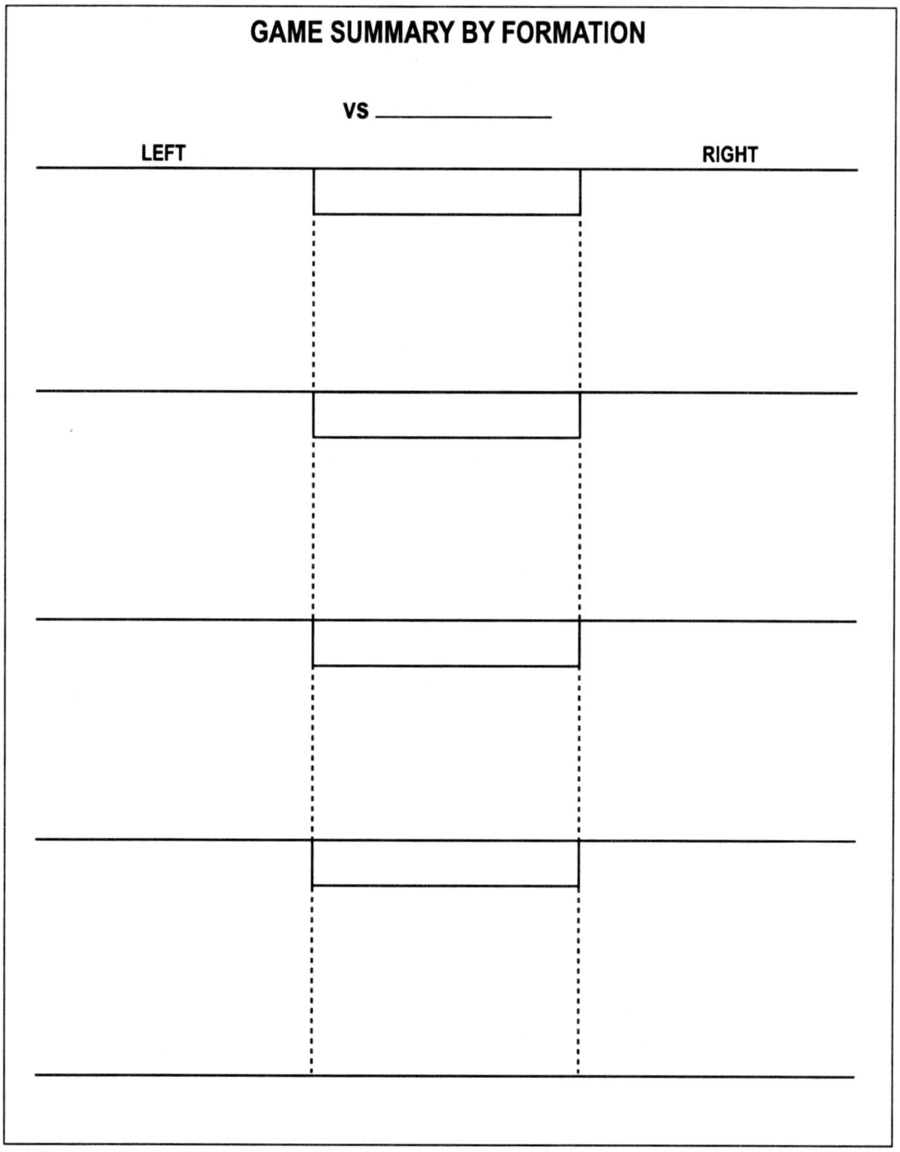

GAME SUMMARY BY FORMATION

VS _____

LEFT | RIGHT

Diagram 6-14. Game summary by formation chart

7

Mini-Topics

The following mini-topics are very important in the development and execution of an explosive offense:

- Throwing on first down
- Establishing an effective running game
- Throwing to the backs
- Utilizing screens/draws/specials
- Recognizing pre-snap coverage
- Attacking zone coverages
- Attacking man coverages
- Getting the ball into playmakers' hands
- Handling blitz situations
- Performing the scramble drill
- Grading/evaluating players
- Focusing on selected game day situations

Throwing on First Down

Many advantages exist when throwing on first down. Most offenses have a goal of gaining four or more yards on first down. Therefore, the style of pass should be of a very high percentage; three-step passing and play action are usual favorites. First down is also a great opportunity to throw the long ball to stretch the defense and send a message. First down is often the most passive down for many defenses, and also the most predictable.

Establishing an Effective Running Game

An effective running game should involve several considerations, one of the most important being how the running game is designed. Running the football involves relying on numbers and angles. Therefore, the offense should focus on formations with one or more of the following advantageous factors:
- A numerical advantage at the point of attack
- Blocking angles that enhance the player's ability to cut off or move his opponent
- The creation of defensive hesitation in reading the play (e.g., lots of formations, pre-snap movement)
- Slowed support of the defensive backs (through the development of a complimentary play action pass scheme)

The kinds of blocking schemes used in an offensive system have an effect on the types of plays that are included in a running game plan. Most offenses incorporate some form of man or zone blocking schemes.

Man schemes take advantage of the one-on-one match-ups by isolating blockers on single defenders. Zone schemes require blockers to control an area of the defensive front rather than a specific man. As a result, a blocker is able to control a defender who is moving through a particular area of the blocker's control. Zone blocking schemes allow blockers in the running game to account for a more active defensive front or shaded defensive alignments. The following are examples of both zone- and man-blocking run plays.

Inside Zone Blocking Play

The ballcarrier is given a single defensive lineman off of whom to make his cut. The offensive line and tight end will use the zone blocking scheme. The running back will read the first down lineman from the center over. Power-slips are used playside and power-scoops are used backside. Generally, this will be a cutback play, but it can also be a run to the weak side. It is preferable to run this at the 3 technique, but it is not necessary.

Assignments:

BST: Scoop B gap to W.

BSG: Power-scoop with C, N to M.

C: Power-scoop with BSG, N to M.

PSG: Power-punch and grab. You are on an island with a 3 technique.

PST: Power-slip. Jab-step toward the end; if the end doesn't come to you, go on up to the safety.

TE: Power-punch and grab. Go up to the safety only if the end crashes into the C gap.

H: Choke the backside Z gap. Stay on the first-level defender for the cutback.

X: Convoy/stalk.

Z: Convoy/stalk.

QB: Open—get the ball to back as deep as possible. Set up or carry out the naked fake.

FB: Open cross-over plant to a width behind the playside tackle. Be patient.

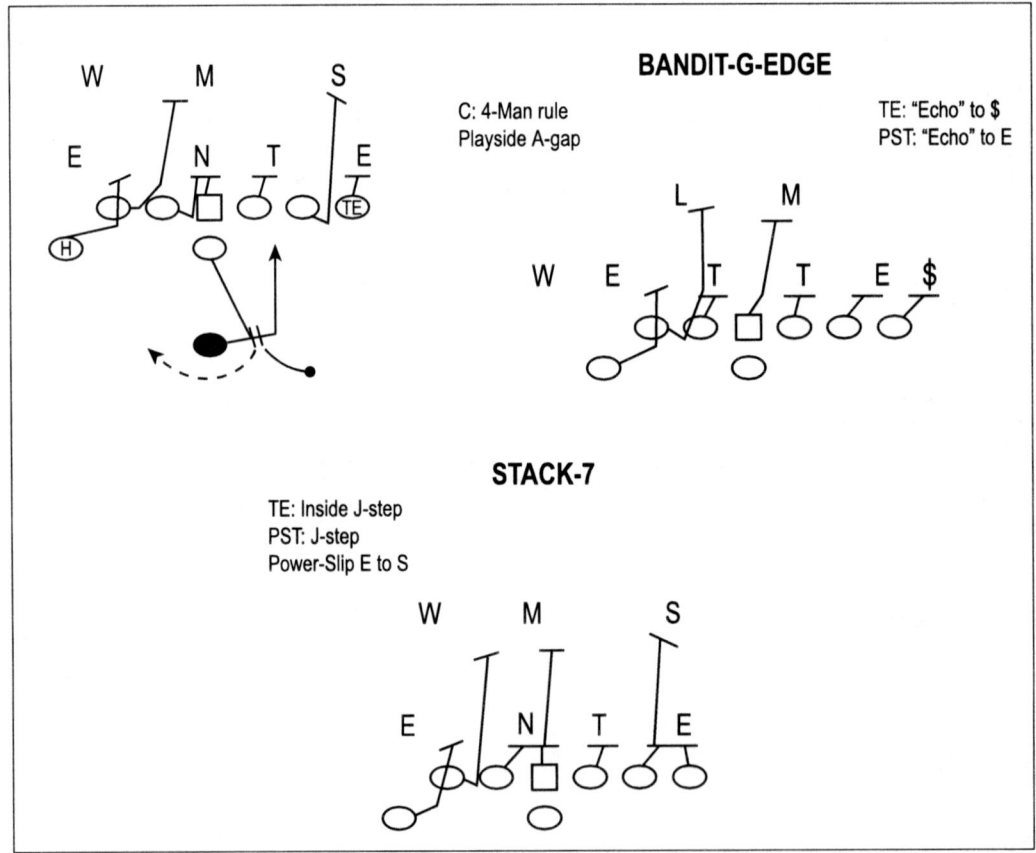

Diagram 7-1. Inside zone blocking play

Counter

The counter is the misdirection counter gap play. A double-team will exist on the playside. The BSG will trap-pull and the BST will power-pull. The center will always seal backside. The tight end will either rip-slam or trey. On the scissors play, the fullback will seal the backside B gap. The halfback will receive the ball, read the BST's power-pull, and run to daylight. On the counter play, the single-back (fullback) will jab-fake, run his track, and take the hand-off. This play can also go weak.

Assignments:

BST: Power-pull.

BSG: Trap-pull.

C: Seal.

PSG: Seal or deuce.

PST: Deuce or trey.

TE: Trey or rip-slam.

H: Lateral step sideways, pick up outside tackle, and stay on outside hip.

X: Convoy.

Z: Convoy.

QB: Execute backfield action—carry out the naked fake.

FB: Position cutoff.

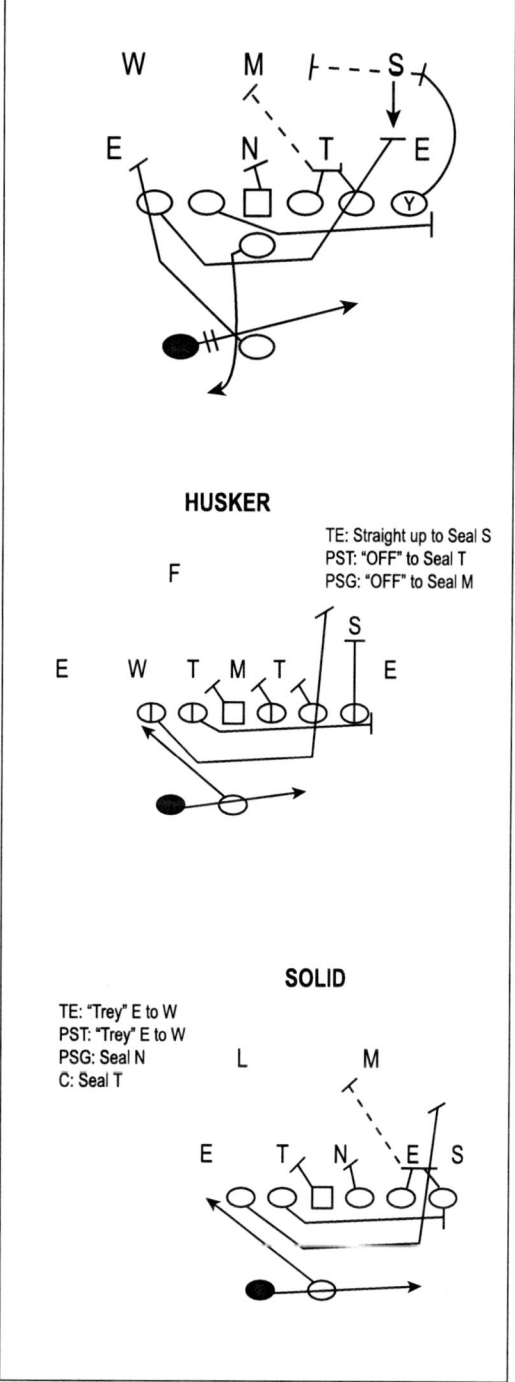

Diagram 7-2. Counter

Lead Draw

This play is designed to take advantage of a hard pass rush by defensive linemen and linebackers dropping into pass coverage. The lead draw features a lead blocking back on the weakside, who must follow a few rules: always kick out edge pressure; if the guard is covered, take a balance step and lead up; if the guard is uncovered, lead up the B gap for wing. The halfback should draw action, hit up the B gap, and run to daylight.

Assignments:

BST: Loop to S.

BSG: Seal T.

C: Loop to M.

PSG: Seal N.

PST: Kick-step to scoop.

TE: Side-step to $.

H: Lead blocker.

X: Stalk.

Z: Stalk.

QB: Dropback hand-off, set up, sell the pass.

FB: Slide. Execute the draw. Read the first down lineman.

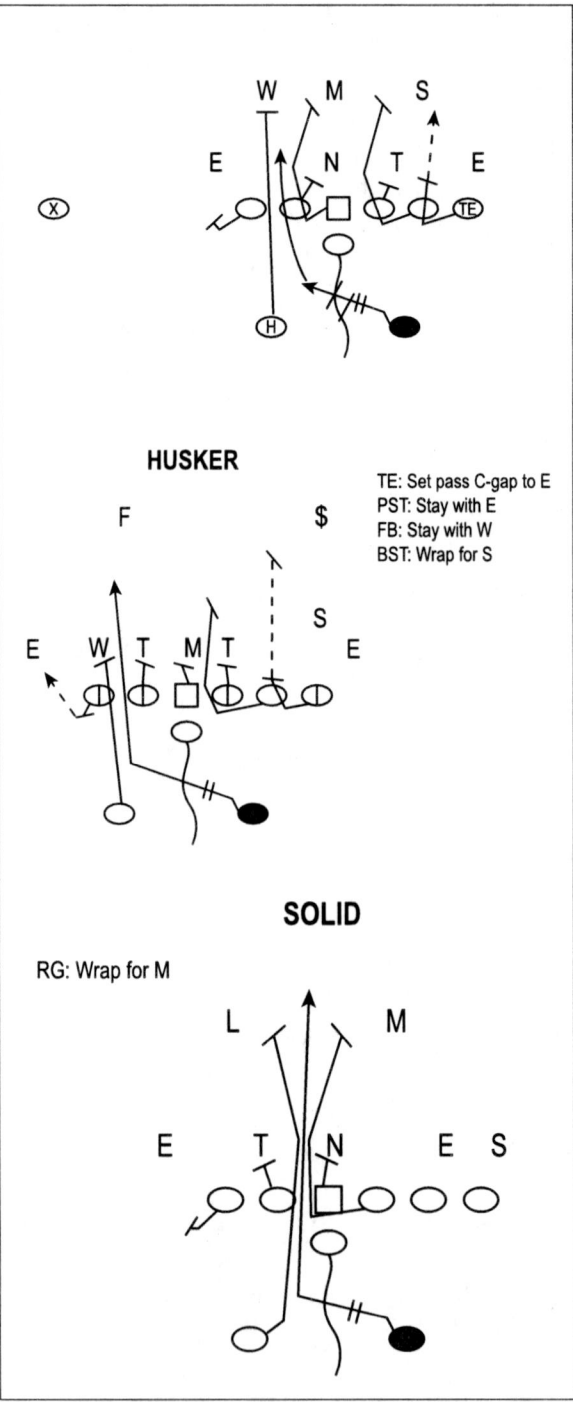

Diagram 7-3. Lead draw

Zone Right, Reverse Left

This play is a misdirection play off of the inside zone run fake. It is a good play versus quick flowing defenses.

Assignments:

LT: Seal inside gap. Flat pull to block support.

LG: Seal inside gap. 45-degree angle pull block flow.

C: Combo with right guard.

RG: Combo with center.

RT: Combo with tight end.

Y: Combo with right tackle.

X: Push-crack the near safety.

Z: Convoy block to near safety.

F (third wide receiver): Jab step. Execute reverse track.

H: Execute inside zone track. Carry out the fake.

QB: Fake inside zone. Execute pitch to fullback on reverse.

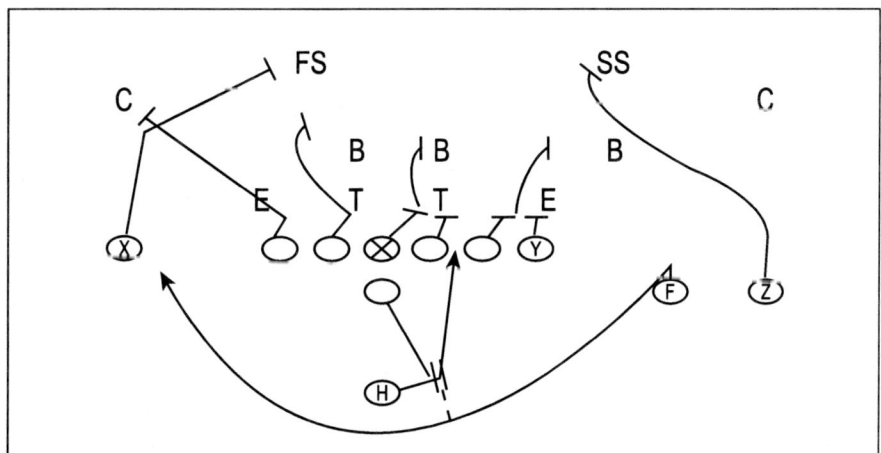

Diagram 7-4. Zone Right, Reverse Left

Throwing to the Backs

Throwing to the running backs is necessary for a complete passing attack for the following reasons:

- Throws to the running backs are high-percentage passes (see running back pass routes).
- Zone coverage defenses will give up the underneath throw to the running backs.
- Versus man coverage, a mismatch is created with a linebacker covering a back (advantage offense).
- Many short passes can be classified as "extended handoffs."
- Running backs are great at advancing the ball after the catch and contact.

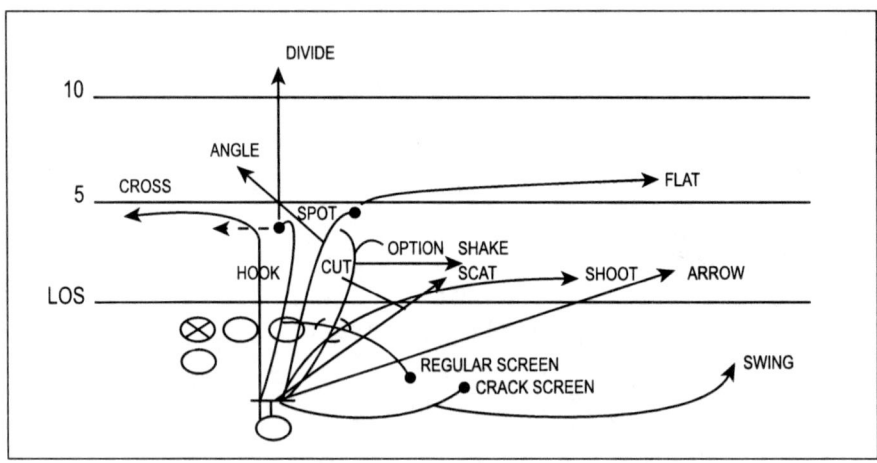

Diagram 7-5. Running Back Pass Routes

Utilizing Screens/Draws/Specials

An offense must have diversity and variety to be effective. Screens, draws, and special plays meet this criterion.

Screens

This style of play is very good at slowing down an aggressive pass rush. Some screen plays are designed to attack zone coverages, and others to exploit man/blitz coverage. It is important to execute a variety of screens to all potential receivers (running back, tight end, wide receiver, and even back to the quarterback). A coach should be careful not to overuse a particular screen or it will lose its effectiveness.

Draws

This style of play is excellent versus an aggressive, out-of-control pass rush when the defensive line does not stay in their rush lanes. Draws are most effective on passing-down situations. The purpose of the draw is to slow down the pass rush.

Specials

Special plays are another way to put the ball into a playmaker's hand and exploit overreacting defenses.

In addition, special plays:
- Can be the difference between a win and a loss.
- Can jump-start the offense.
- Can score a touchdown off of one play (or create a big play).
- Are exciting to practice and execute in the game.
- Are great for fans.

Pre-Snap Coverage Recognition

In a passing offense, it is important to get all five potential receivers into a pass route as often as possible. For an offense to be most effective, the quarterback and all possible receivers must see and recognize the coverage.

It is important to have a thorough understanding of coverages in general, and more important to understand the anticipated coverage of a specific opponent. This is a difficult task because defenses may use multiple coverages that at times utilize five, six, and seven defensive backs. In addition, defenses disguise coverages. However, the task is made easier if the offensive personnel recognize that each pass coverage has some basic philosophies, principles, and priorities. The first responsibility of secondary personnel should be to defend against the pass. This includes preventing the long scoring pass. After this goal is secured, support versus running plays becomes the top priority.

As a unit, the defensive secondary basically relies on either a zone coverage in which each member defends an area of the field, or a man-to-man coverage in which each member defends against a particular eligible receiver. A combination can exist where some players are in zone coverage and others are in man coverage. Coverages can be combined in a variety of ways to accomplish defensive goals.

Many defenses attempt to disguise and vary coverages throughout the course of the game to make it more difficult for the offense to recognize the coverage and make the proper adjustments. Certain pass patterns have a greater chance of success if they are utilized against specific coverages.

If the offense anticipates a specific coverage, the opportunity to call successful plays is greater. When the quarterback "reads" a specific coverage he can use the audible system to change a play at the line of scrimmage.

If the defense is successful in confusing the quarterback and the receivers by showing various coverages or changing the coverage at the last possible second, the chances for a successful play are lessened. The defense has a greater ability to cover the pass pattern if confusion exists regarding where the receivers should be and where the quarterback thinks the secondary personnel will be.

Cover Zone

3	=	3 deep/4 under (4-man rush)
2	=	2 deep/5 under (4-man rush)
4	=	4 deep/3 under (4-man rush)
6	=	Q/Q/half/4 under (4-man rush)
83	=	3 deep/5 under (3-man rush) prevent defense
82	=	2 deep/6 under (3-man rush) prevent defense
84	=	4 deep/4 under (3-man rush) prevent defense

Cover (Man)

1	=	Man/free safety
9	=	Man/no free safety
1 combo	=	Bracket/free safety involved in bracket (treat line 1)
2 deep man under	=	2 deep safeties/man underneath
0	=	Blitz cover (8-man blitz)
Blitz	=	DB or secondary rush
Dog	=	Linebacker rushing
Bear	=	Press look over tight end by a DB or linebacker
Nickel	=	5 DBs in game
Dime	=	6 DBs in game
Press	=	Another term for bump and run (may cause wide receiver to adjust route)
Zombie	=	Term added to coverage call signifying zone blitz
Lurk	=	Linebacker(s) as a hole player
Robber	=	Safety as a hole player

Note: Double digits signify nickel back in game. Example: cover 33 (cover 3 with 5 DBs).

Diagram 7-6. Coverage terminology

The offense, in preparing for an opponent, should know the coverages they anticipate seeing and spend the majority of practice time against these coverages. If the receivers and quarterback do this diligently, the opportunities for success and the chances of throwing completed passes are enhanced. Clearly, the chances for victory also are greater. Diagrams 7-6 through 7-11 illustrate the basic man and zone pass coverages and variations.

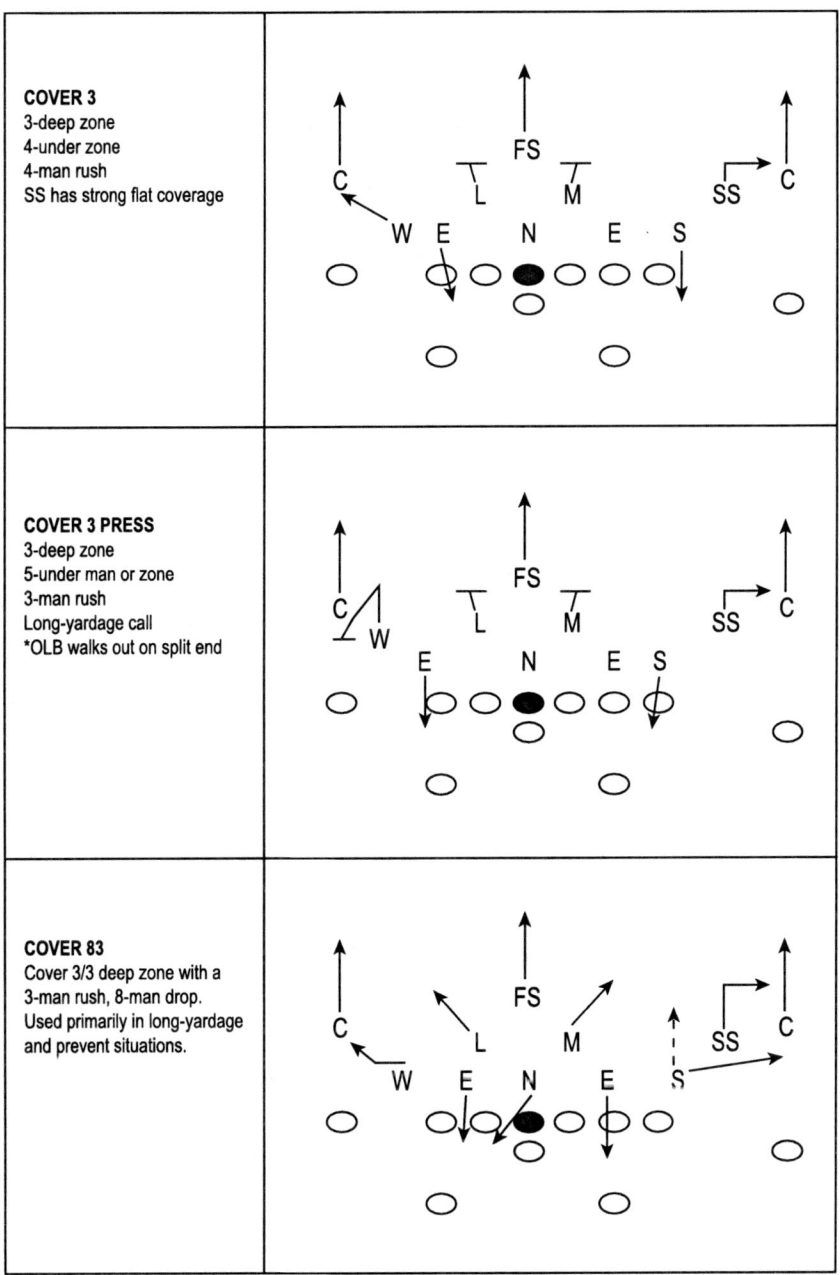

Diagram 7-7. Cover 3 (3 deep zone) and variations

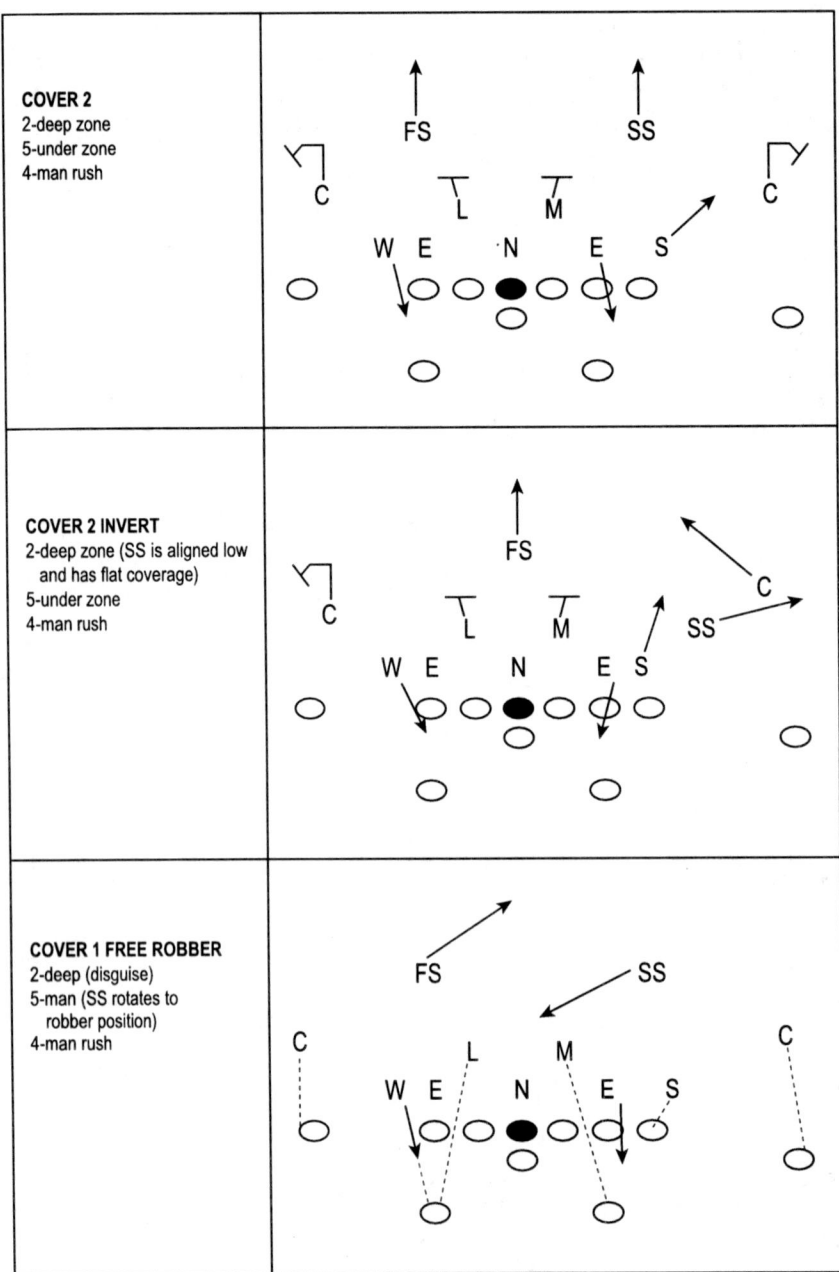

Diagram 7-8. Cover 2 (2 deep zone) and variations

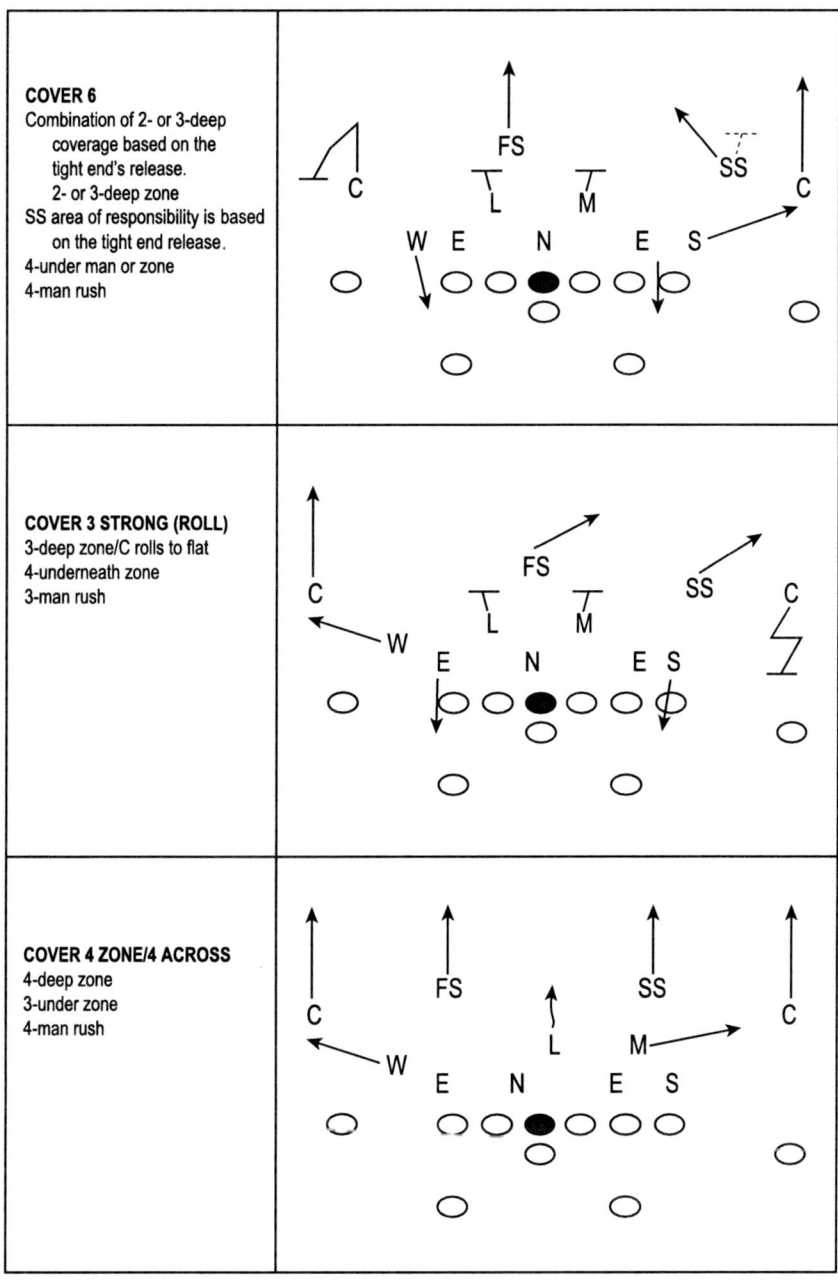

Diagram 7-9. Quarters/roll weak/roll strong and variations

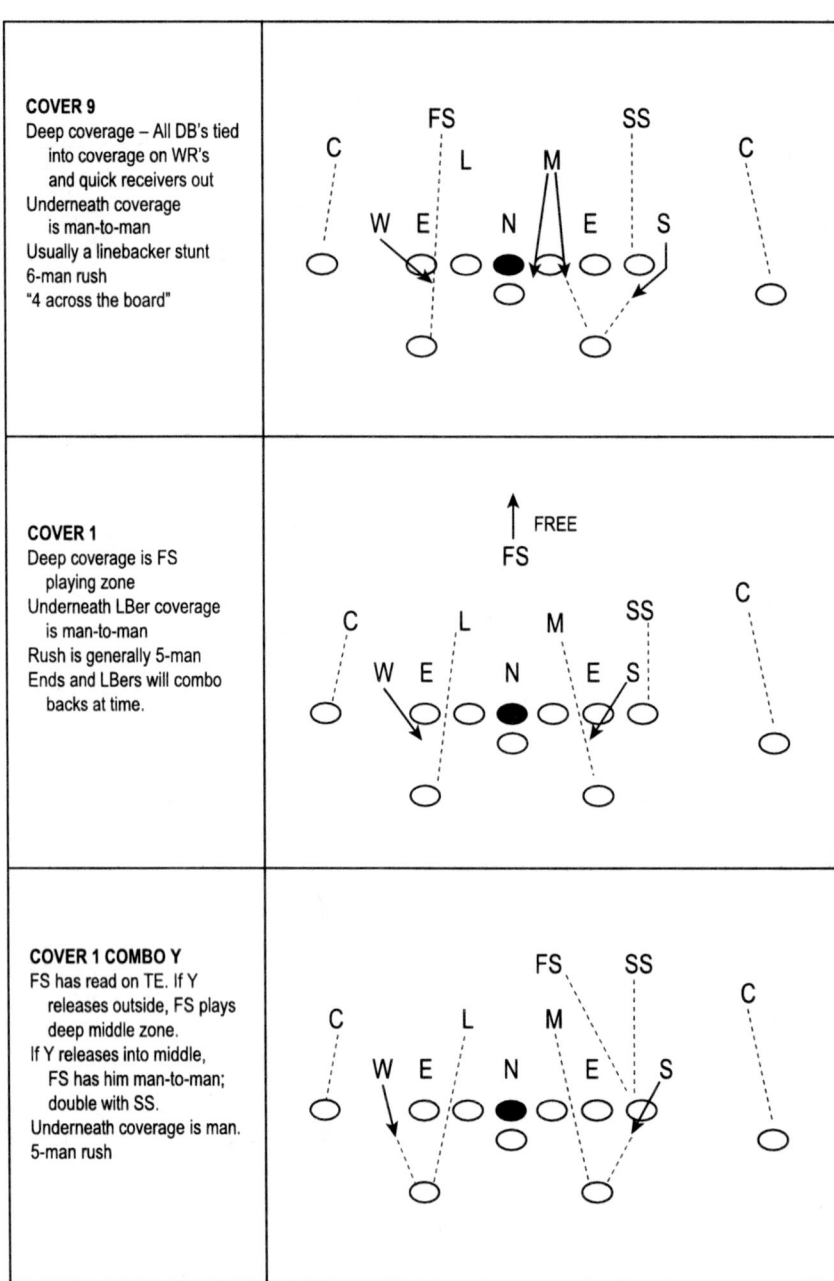

Diagram 7-10. Man coverage

COVER 9
Deep coverage – All DB's tied into coverage on WR's and quick receivers out
Underneath coverage is man-to-man
Usually a linebacker stunt
6-man rush
"4 across the board"

COVER 1
Deep coverage is FS playing zone
Underneath LBer coverage is man-to-man
Rush is generally 5-man
Ends and LBers will combo backs at time.

COVER 1 COMBO Y
FS has read on TE. If Y releases outside, FS plays deep middle zone.
If Y releases into middle, FS has him man-to-man; double with SS.
Underneath coverage is man.
5-man rush

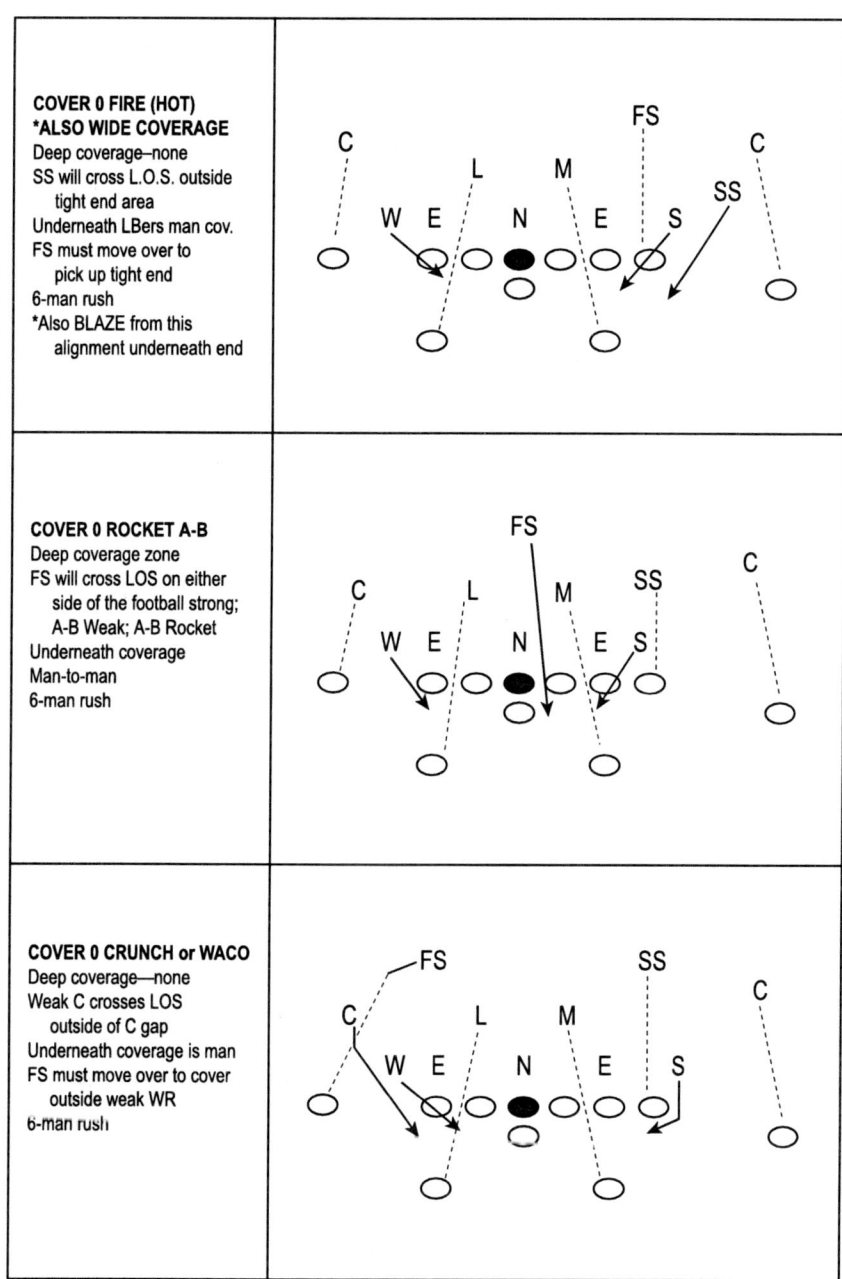

Diagram 7-11. Cover zero (man) with blitz

COVER 0 FIRE (HOT)
***ALSO WIDE COVERAGE**
Deep coverage–none
SS will cross L.O.S. outside tight end area
Underneath LBers man cov.
FS must move over to pick up tight end
6-man rush
*Also BLAZE from this alignment underneath end

COVER 0 ROCKET A-B
Deep coverage zone
FS will cross LOS on either side of the football strong; A-B Weak; A-B Rocket
Underneath coverage
Man-to-man
6-man rush

COVER 0 CRUNCH or WACO
Deep coverage—none
Weak C crosses LOS outside of C gap
Underneath coverage is man
FS must move over to cover outside weak WR
6-man rush

Steps to be Taken in Pre-Snap Reads

- Locate the safeties (both the free and strong safety)
- Read the alignment of the free safety:
  - ✓ Position #1 = weakside and up
  - ✓ Position #2 = weakside and deep
  - ✓ Position #3 = near the middle one-third and deep
  - ✓ Position #4 = strongside and up (on tight end)

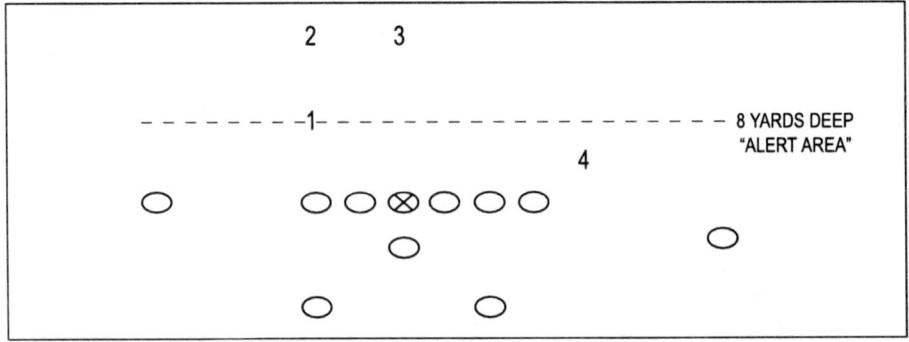

Diagram 7-12. Location of the safeties

What the Alignment of the Free Safety Tells the Quarterback and Receivers

Position #1 Possibilities

- Cover zero (man with no free safety; free safety M/M on #2 receiver weak).
- Cover zero (free safety blitz).

Position #2 Possibilities

- Cover 2 (2 deep with 5 under zone). Giveaways are the corners; if they are on the outside shoulder of the wide receiver and looking in to the quarterback it is usually 2 deep zone.
- Cover 2 (2 deep with 5 under man). Giveaways are the corners; if they are on the inside shoulder of the wide receiver it is usually cover 2 man (possibly cover 1 combo).

Note: The corners may line up head-up on the wide receivers and take a side on the snap.

- Cover 4 (weak roll) (3 deep with corner rotation weak). Giveaway is the alignment and movement on the snap of the strong safety; if he goes to the middle deep one-third, it is usually cover 4 weak roll. If he goes to the hash area it is usually cover 2.

Position #3 Possibilities

- Cover 3/3C (3 deep with 4 under zone; SS-safety rotation weak). Giveaway is the alignment and movement of the strong safety; if he is outside of the tight end and five to six yards deep and goes to the flat on the snap, it is cover 3SS. If he is slightly deeper, and goes to the deep outside one-third on the snap, it is cover 3C.
- Cover 83 or 3-5-3 (3 deep with 5 under zone). It is the same as 3SS/3C but with an additional defender in the underneath coverage.
- Cover 1-man with one free safety. Giveaway is the alignment and movement of the strong safety; if he is lined up on the tight end and is not too deep, it is usually cover 1 (he will eyeball the tight end and cover him on the snap).

Note: The free safety may play games by moving back and forth between the #2 and #3 positions. The weak outside linebacker can sometimes be a clue of whether it is cover 2 or cover 3; if he is in a walking position, it is usually cover 3 and if he is on the tackle, it is usually cover 2 or cover 4.

Position #4 Possibilities

- Cover zero/SS blitz-FS man-to-man on the #2 receiver strong.

Note: The free safety may play games by moving back and forth between #3 and #4 position.

The Progression in Reading Coverages

- Locate the safeties to make sure the quarterback is protected.
- Locating the position of the free safety will help minimize the possible coverages that could be executed from that position.
- At the snap, the quarterback's eyes should be focused on the strong safety during the first few steps of the backpedal to verify the actual coverage.

Note: The receivers and running back should also recognize the coverage and make the proper route adjustments.

Important Factors to Consider in Attacking the Coverage

- Defender freelancing (not playing his position in a disciplined manner).
- Mismatches (great receiver on poor defender).
- Utilizing motions and multiple formations may cause confusion or force defenders to play out of position.

Attacking Zone Coverages

When attacking zone coverages, it is important to use patterns that stretch defenses and find the soft spots. The pass plays should be designed to stretch the defense vertically or horizontally. Diagrams 7-13 and 7-14 display areas to attack in basic zone coverages. (Weaknesses are identified by diagonal lines).

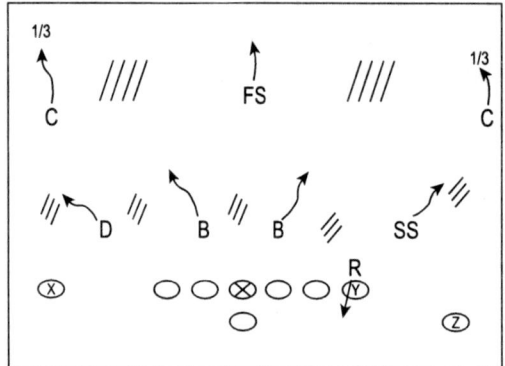

Diagram 7-13. Cover 3 (3 deep/4 underneath zone)

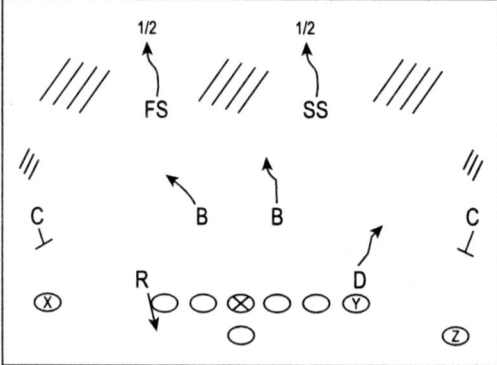

Diagram 7-14. Cover 2 (2 deep/5 underneath zone)

Attacking Man Coverages

When attacking man coverages, it is important to use patterns with definite breaks and acceleration points. The offensive system should allow the quarterback to look for mismatches in personnel and have a selection of plays that will attack that specific weakness. Crossing routes can be very effective because they may cause defensive confusion and natural picks. Diagrams 7-15 and 7-16 display man-to-man coverages.

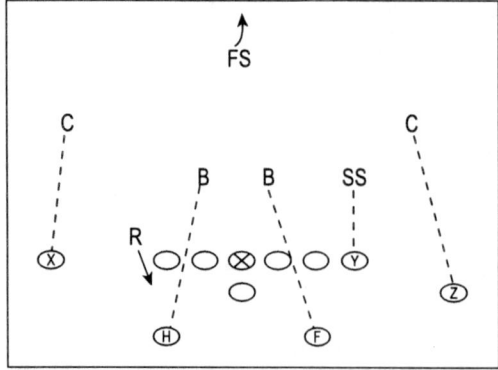

Diagram 7-15. Man coverage with a free safety

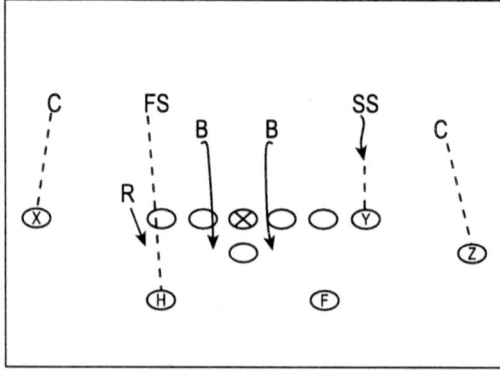

Diagram 7-16. Man coverage—no free safety

Getting the Ball into Playmakers' Hands

When developing the offensive plan, it is important to identify the team's playmakers, the athletes who must have the ball in their hands a major portion of the game for the team to be successful. The playmaker title is earned through hard work and production in practice and games. Many successful coaches design specific plays beyond the core offense to allow these gifted athletes to use their skills. A good idea during games is to assign a specific coach (in the press box) to chart the number of touches the playmakers have to ensure that the offense will not get off course.

Handling Blitz Situations

If an offense demonstrates that it cannot handle blitz/pressure situations by the defense, they can count on seeing it down after down. Therefore, it is important for the entire offense (all 11 men) to realize that each has a specific job to do. It is important to put the team in game-like blitz situations in practice sessions and make it very difficult for the offense. Each player should understand the pass-protection scheme, read keys in defensive coverage to anticipate the blitz, and make the proper sight adjustments or hot reads. Defensive coaches have become increasingly more effective in disguising the blitz by showing blitz, then bluffing and dropping back into a basic zone coverage. Therefore, instead of using blitz audibles (changing the play at the line of scrimmage) many offenses will now spread the field with formations to get a definite tip or pre-snap read on the coverage.

Performing the Scramble Drill

The execution of any offense is always far from perfect. A scrambling quarterback is usually an indication that an offensive breakdown has occurred. It is important to establish guidelines for the quarterback to follow in this situation to salvage a positive outcome on the play. When a quarterback is forced out of the pocket, his receivers also have additional adjustments they should make.

Basic Scramble Rules

- Receivers' adjustment when the quarterback scrambles are as follows:
- Quarterback runs toward (no sideline): run away (take off).
- Quarterback runs toward (sideline available): run with the quarterback at route depth.
- Quarterback runs away (replace at route depth).
- Quarterback scrambles up the middle: receivers in the middle run away; others work their way between hashes.

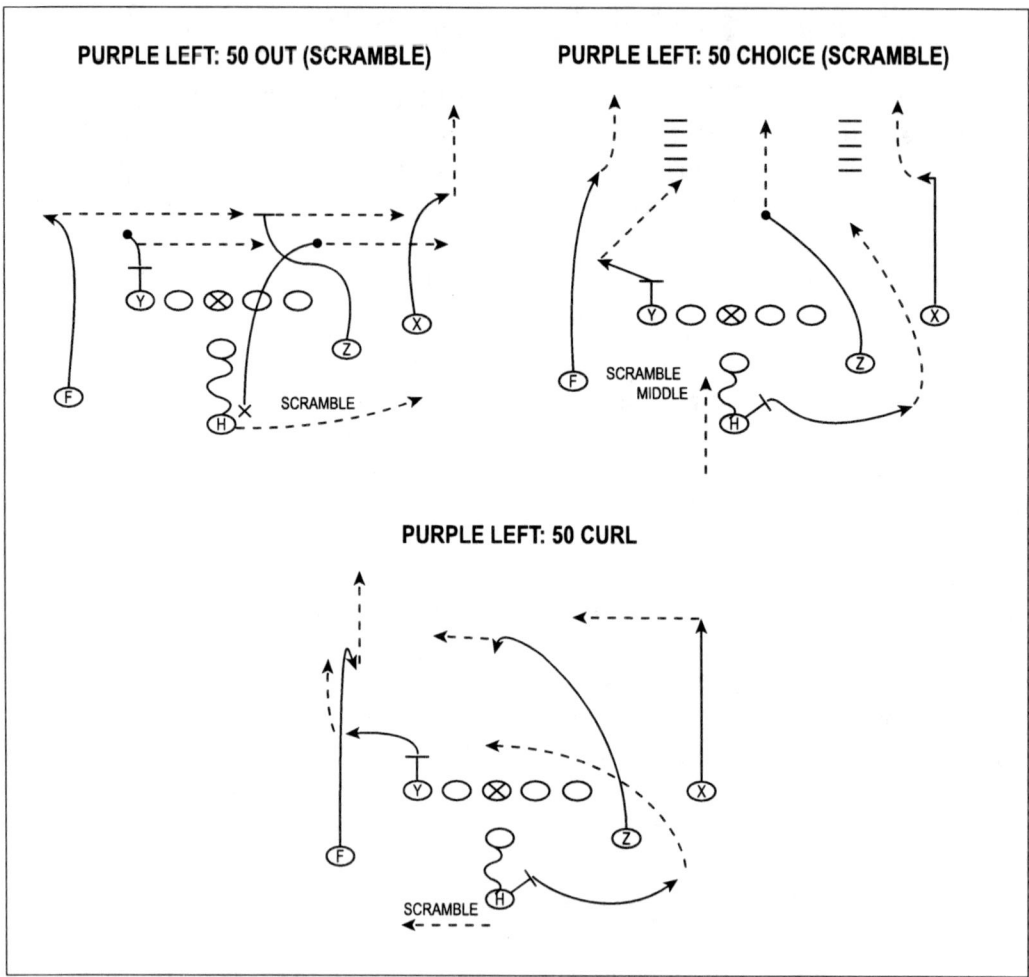

Diagram 7-17. Scramble drill

Grading/Evaluating Players

Grading and evaluating players is a great method of motivation. All of the players should be held accountable for their performance. The evaluations are also important for gathering information and keeping proper records because tough coaching decisions need to be made (e.g. who is first offense, second offense).

Criteria for Grading Wide Receivers

Effort

- Chart loafs and great efforts

Execution

- Chart missed assignments
- Technique and fundamentals: routes and releases

Production

- Chart catches and drops
- YAC—yards after the catch
- Big-play capability
  - ✓ Chart catches and drops
  - ✓ Circus catches (making the impossible possible)
- Blocking

Criteria for Evaluating Quarterbacks

Statistics and general comments (grading) should be noted for each quarterback after each practice session. The quarterbacks will be evaluated and are accountable for their performance. Each snap must be valued.

Meetings—Student of the Game

- Studying playbook/video
- Note taking
- Responses (Q/A)
- Oral/written tests

Practices

- Fundamentals/techniques
- Drill work (decision-making and execution)
  - ✓ Inside (running game)
  - ✓ Team
  - ✓ Skeleton
- Situations (how does he respond?)
  - ✓ Red zone
  - ✓ Blitz
  - ✓ No huddle
  - ✓ Two minute

- Scrimmages
    - ✓ Executing the offensive system
    - ✓ Ball security—no turnovers
    - ✓ Finish drives—making big plays when they present themselves

Selected Game-Day Situations

Each game-day situation involves very specific conditions in which down and distance and field position are critically important to play selection.

Normal Down Offense

Moving the chains (i.e., getting first downs) on first and second down is the mark of a good offense. Most attention on first and 10 should be on positioning the offense in a favorable down and distance situation for second down. An efficient level of success on first down is four-plus yards. First down success will be a major factor affecting the outcome of the game.

Third Down Offense

Most teams have very specific tendencies with regard to their defensive package and strategy on third down. Therefore, an offense should be able to select the best plays with which to attack the defense and convert the first down.
- Third and long (seven-plus yards)
- Third and medium (two to six yards)
- Third and short (one yard or less)

Most offenses will have 12 to 14 crucial third down situations in a game. The longer the yardage situations, the lower the chances are of conversion. An offense that converts 45% or greater will be very successful.

The Red Zone Offense

Review the following priorities of a productive red zone offense:
- Run the football—make sure to not run plays that risk losing yards.
- Utilize motion and formations to create the desired match-ups in the passing game.
- Pass plays should be designed to beat the blitz and man coverage.
- Pass the ball to underneath routes (crossing patterns are good).
- The offense should not be taken out of field goal range. Negative yardage plays (e.g., sacks) and turnovers should not happen because the offense is already in scoring territory.

The Four-Minute Offense

The primary goal of the four-minute offense is to take as much time off the clock as possible, while enabling a team to protect its lead. The four objectives of the four-minute offense include:

- Move the ball with run plays
- Make first downs
- Keep the clock running
- Protect the football

The Two-Minute Offense

The two-minute offense is designed to enable a team to score either a touchdown or field goal within the limited amount of time available. The offense should have the ability to activate the two-minute offense within the body of a drive, or initiate it as a beginning series.

The two-minute offense activated prior to the end of the first half is usually intended to get the team into position for a medium-range field goal. If the two-minute drill is utilized near the end of the game, the objective is usually to secure whatever points are needed for a win or at least a tie.

Two-Minute Offense Procedures and Strategy

The two-minute offense mode will be either a sideline or huddle call. The quarterback will direct all offensive procedures but the entire offense must be alert to this situation. Note: Time is a factor, so a definite sense of urgency exists. But remember, the offense should also be poised.

Methods of Stopping the Game Clock (Know the Rules of the Game!)

- Time-out
- Incomplete pass
- Out of bounds
- Change of possession
- Penalty (after the mark off, the clock starts)
- Injury (clock re-starts after the injured player leaves the field)
- First down (after the chains are set, the clock starts)

General Ballcarrier Guidelines

- Always advance the ball as far as possible, but get out of bounds (save time-outs). The exception is when picking up a definite first down.

- Know the down/distance—be smart.
- The quarterback should never take a sack. Incompletes are OK (except on fourth down).
- After being tackled inbounds, hustle to get up quickly and give the ball to an official.

Time-outs

Time-outs are precious, so you should always value them. The quarterback (or other designated offensive player) will call a time-out only by direction from the sideline coach(es).

In certain situations, all offensive players may come to the sideline to receive instructions during time-outs. When the offense is on the sideline, utilize the sideline huddle, and then break and hustle to the line of scrimmage to run the next play.

Special Terms

- Subway—Alerts the center and offensive line that the quarterback will align underneath the center.
- Clock—Automatic quick out route to gain yards plus stop the clock (no exceptions).

    Cadence: "Clock—clock-set-hut." The line uses field goal protection. The quarterback must get the completion or throw the ball away (incomplete).

- Kill—Quarterback spikes the football to stop the clock.

    Cadence: "Kill—kill-set-hut."

Situations

Bulls-eye

Bulls-eye is an offensive function that will allow the quarterback to center the ball in the middle of the hashes to enhance the field goal accuracy. The quarterback will call "bulls-eye right" or "left" and all skilled positions will align on the line of scrimmage in the direction called to build a wall. The quarterback will receive the snap, run to the middle location, and try to minimize the number of yards lost.

Red Field Goal

This is a hurry-up field goal situation used mostly on fourth down with no time-outs remaining. When the offensive players not involved on the field goal team hear "red field goal," they immediately sprint to the sideline. Or, if field goal personnel are on the sideline when "red field goal" is called, they immediately sprint onto the field and line up in their field goal positions.

Personnel/Formations

- Flush (four wide receivers/one running back)
- Diamond (three wide receivers/one running back/one tight end)
- Automatic slot by tight end unless "subway" is called.
- Purple (slot)

Note: Other formations/motions can be used on a huddle call.

Two-Minute Offense: Ready List (Tentative)

Runs

Zone (4/5)
Draw (0/1)
Situations
Clock
Kill
Subway

Three-Step Series

Slant
Hitch
Out
Arrow

Five-Step or Gun Series

Out
Curl
Bench
Smash
Choice
Option
Post dig
Comeback
Takeoff
Post corner
Hail Mary
Sail

Note: Most of the offense can be called during two-minute procedures, but will usually be limited to increase execution.

Procedure for Calling Plays at the Line of Scrimmage

- After the previous play, the quarterback will immediately make a strength call (right or left). This will set the formation and placement of Y (tight end). The wide receivers will already know the formation alignment that will be used during this particular drive.
  - ✓ Example: Purple—The formation can be changed during a drive by the quarterback. The outside wide receivers should be interchangeable in most formations to save time. Personnel will change only in huddle situations, but formation alignment may change during a two-minute drive.

- The quarterback will receive signals for the play or formation change from the sideline. The quarterback will be prepared to call a specific play or plays on his own in emergency situations.
- The quarterback will communicate his location, either gun or subway, to the center and line.
- Cadence
  - ✓ Gun—The quarterback will call out the play and use hand signals to the wide receivers. A silent "on one" snap count will be used. However, the silent snap count can be a change-up on a game-by-game basis.
  - ✓ Subway—The quarterback will call out the play and use hand signals to the wide receivers. The snap count is an automatic "on one."

Some examples of special game situations are shown in Diagrams 7-18 through 7-21.

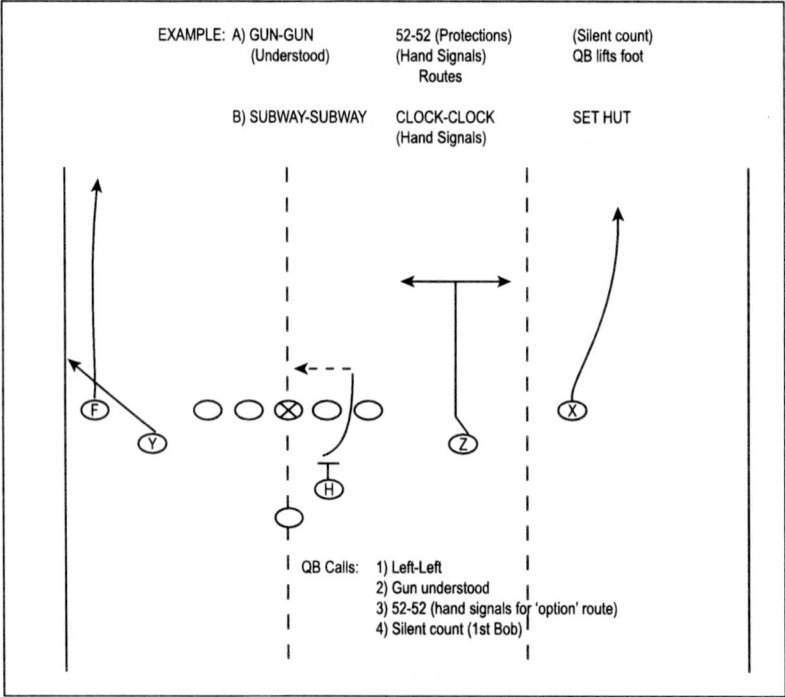

Diagram 7-18. Example play call from the line of scrimmage

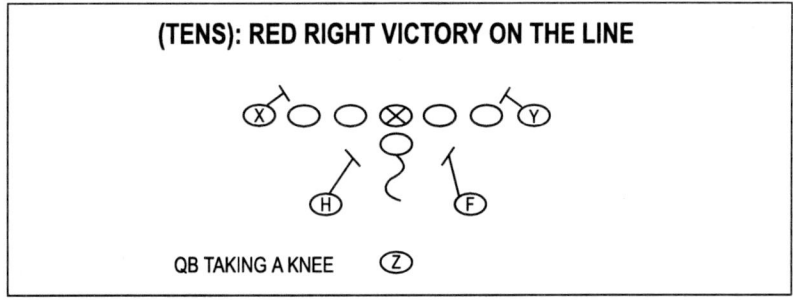

Diagram 7-19. Victory

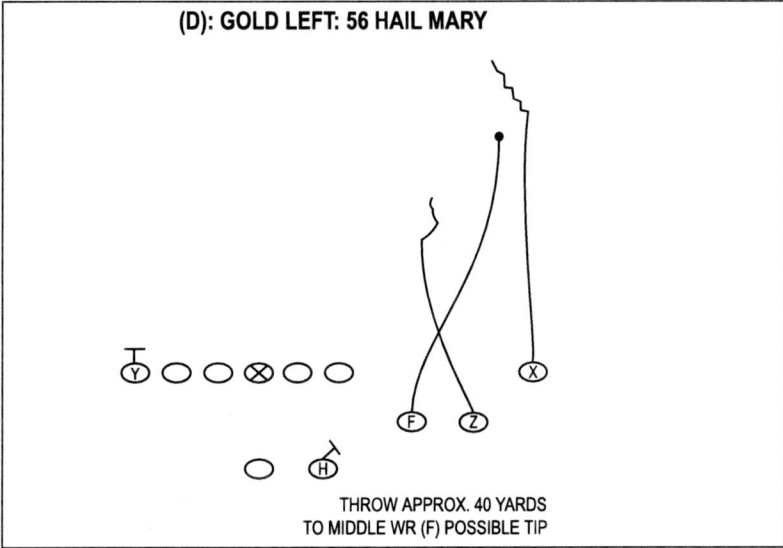

Diagram 7-20. Hail Mary

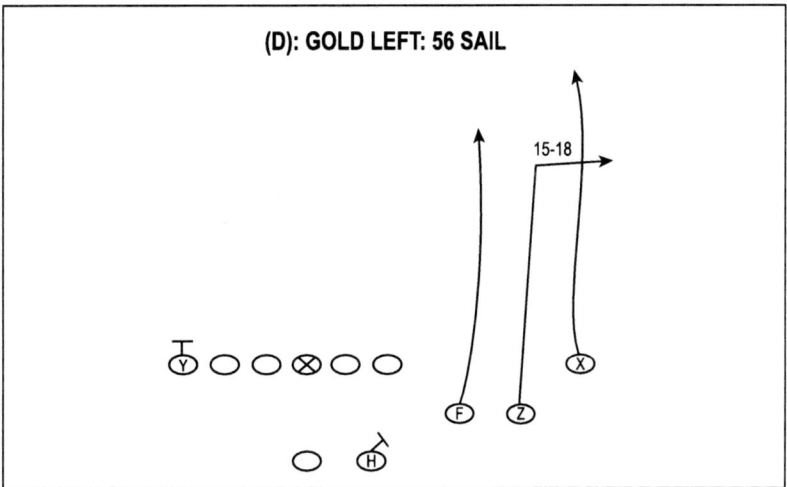

Diagram 7-21. Sail

8

25 Explosive Offensive Plays

Within the weekly offensive game plan, a coach should design explosive plays. These plays can jump-start the offense, and therefore need to be innovative and able to exploit a defensive weakness or defensive player. These plays need to be set up properly and called at the right time.

Numerous factors exist when considering the design of explosive plays, as well as the timing of when they should be called. Considering the following factors can aid coaches in their efforts to develop this unique package.

- Most successful specials complement a core/base offensive play that a team has in its offensive plan.
- Try to use a variety of formations/motions/personnel groupings to help in disguising the play from game to game. Special plays will quickly lose their effectiveness when they are overused.
- A coach should give these plays enough practice preparation. Repetitions are the key to offensive success.
- Timing is paramount. A special play called at the proper time can be the difference between a win or a loss. Also, early in the game is a great opportunity to jump-start an offense.

- Explosive plays are designed to exploit a defense tendency, weakness, or particular player.
- Players make plays. Coaches should put athletes in the best situation possible to utilize their skills and be successful.
- Other factors to consider when game-planning special plays:
  - ✓ Down/distance
  - ✓ Field location: red zone, hash, etc.
  - ✓ Time of game: first/fourth quarter, before half, etc.
  - ✓ Change of possession or after a big play when the defense is rattled or confused

25 Explosive Plays

Load Option I (Gun)

A load option I is a special option play designed to put the ball directly into a playmaker's hand. A gun snap may be safer if the quarterback is not accustomed to taking under-center exchanges. This method will allow an option game, even if the quarterback is limited or should not be exposed to more hits (contact).

Assignments:

Quarterback: Break the huddle; align in the flanker position—opposite of the load option direction.

Flanker (Z): Gun alignment; secure the snap—execute the option; read the first defender outside of the load block on or off the line of scrimmage.

Split end (X): Stalk-block the defender aligned on.

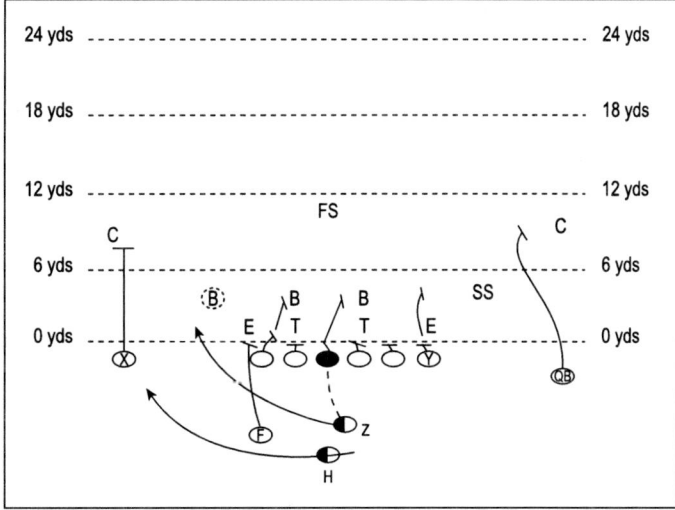

Diagram 8-1. Load option I (gun)

Tight end (Y): Slam—inside release and be in position cut-off the backside pursuit.

Fullback (F): Execute a load block.

Halfback (H): Jab step, arc to keep the proper pitch relationship to Z (flanker).

Load Option II (Handoff)

The load option II is a special option play that can be executed out of various backfield alignments (e.g., power I, T formation). This option has big-play potential by putting the ball into the playmaker's hands and is great in short-yardage or run-down situations.

Assignments:

Quarterback: Reverse out; secure the handoff to Z—carry out a naked fake.

Flanker (Z): Secure the handoff—execute option; read the first defender outside of the load block on or off the line of scrimmage.

Split end (X): Stalk-block the defender aligned on.

Tight end (Y): Slam—inside release and be in position to cut off the backside pursuit.

Fullback (F): Execute a load block.

Halfback (H): Jab step; arc to keep the proper pitch relationship to Z (flanker).

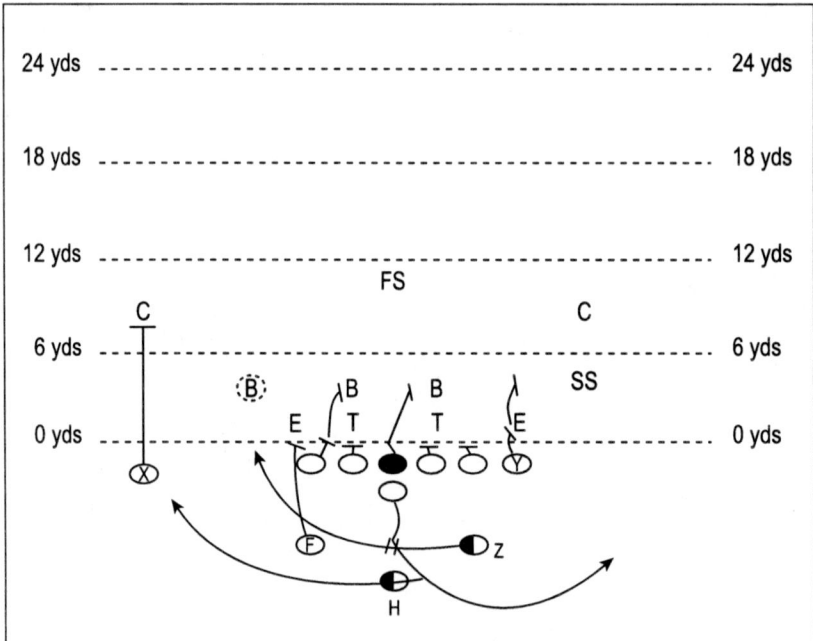

Diagram 8-2. Load option II (handoff)

Hand Sweep

This running play is designed to complement an offense that utilizes flat, wide receiver motion. It is a great opportunity to safely put the ball into a playmaker's hands. A simple blocking scheme should be used—outside zone or stretch. A quick-hitting run, this play can be disguised by utilizing many formations.

Assignments:

Quarterback: Must time motion for the snap; secure the handoff and carry out the speed option fake in the opposite direction.

Flanker (Z): Inside (zing) motion; must time the snap to receive the ball when near full speed.

Split end (X): Convoy block to the far safety.

Tight end (Y): Outside zone or stretch blocking scheme.

Third wide receiver (F): Stalk-block the defender aligned on.

Halfback (H): Counter step; carry out the speed option fake opposite the sweep (run).

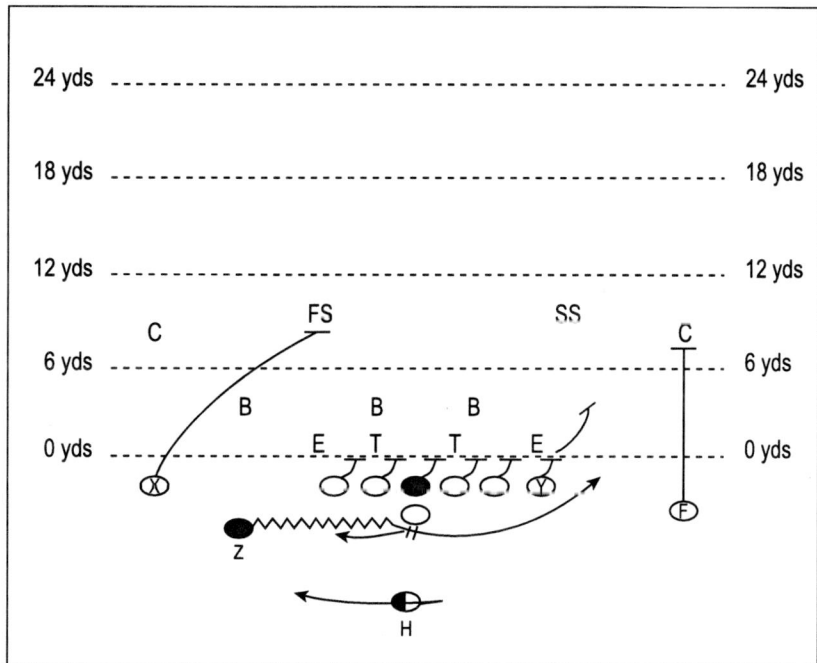

Diagram 8-3. Hand sweep

Pitch

The pitch is a play designed complement the belly or quick-hitting cutback runs. This style of pitch helps protect the quarterback, as opposed to a down-the-line option.

Assignments:

Quarterback: Reverse out—pitch to the halfback (quick).

Flanker (Z): Convoy block to the far safety.

Split end (X): Stalk-block.

Tight end (Y): Slam—release to position for a cut-off block.

Fullback (F): Run a tight belly track; sell the fake on your own.

Halfback (H): Secure the pitch; run to daylight.

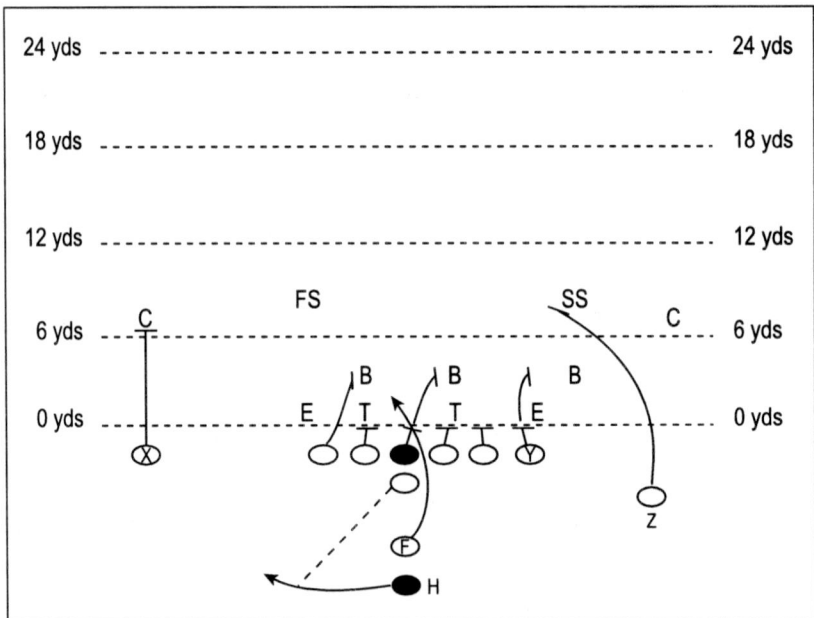

Diagram 8-4. Pitch

Run/Pass Option (Stack the Receivers)

This play allows the quarterback to read the defense by alignment. The play call is zone left (run). The quarterback has the following possibilities:

- If the defense displaces (five in box), run zone left.
- If the defense does not displace (six or more in box), snap the pass to the fullback.
- If the defense aligns in a gray area, read the backside defensive end for give or pull on a run play.

Assignments:

Quarterback: Gun alignment; the read defensive alignment; be patient. This play is great on first-and-10 situations.

Flanker (Z): Stack—block number two—most dangerous defender.

Split end (X): Stack—block number one—most dangerous defender.

Fourth wide receiver (Y): Stalk-block.

Third wide receiver (F): Jab-step; square up to receive a possible pass.

Halfback (H): Align opposite the run call; execute a zone run track; be prepared to receive the ball.

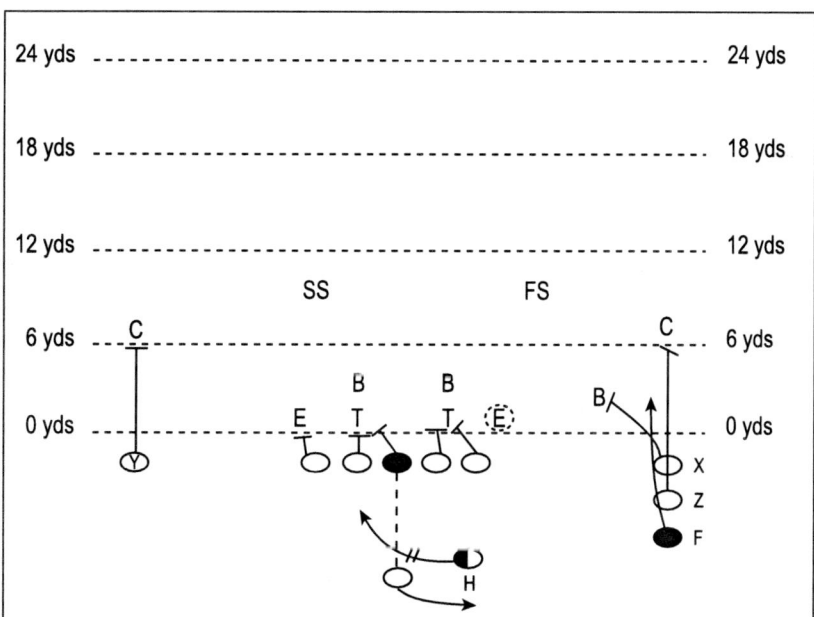

Diagram 8-5. Run/pass option

Quarterback Draw

The quarterback draw can be executed out of numerous formations. Spreading the field (sideline to sideline) allows the quarterback to dictate to the defense. For example, five defenders in box means the offense should execute the quarterback draw, while six or more defenders in the box should tell the quarterback to audible to a pass play or hit the uncovered wide receiver.

Assignments:

Quarterback: Gun or underneath alignment; be patient with the drop—sell the pass. Five in the box, execute the draw; six or more in box, audible to a pass or hit the uncovered wide receiver.

Flanker (Z): Stalk the defender; against man coverage, release outside on a takeoff route.

Split end (X): Stalk the defender; against man coverage, release outside on a takeoff route.

Fourth wide receiver (Y): Stalk the defender; against man coverage, release outside on a takeoff route.

Third wide receiver (F): Stalk the defender; against man coverage, release outside on a takeoff route.

Fifth wide receiver or halfback (H): Stalk the defender; against man coverage, release outside on a takeoff route.

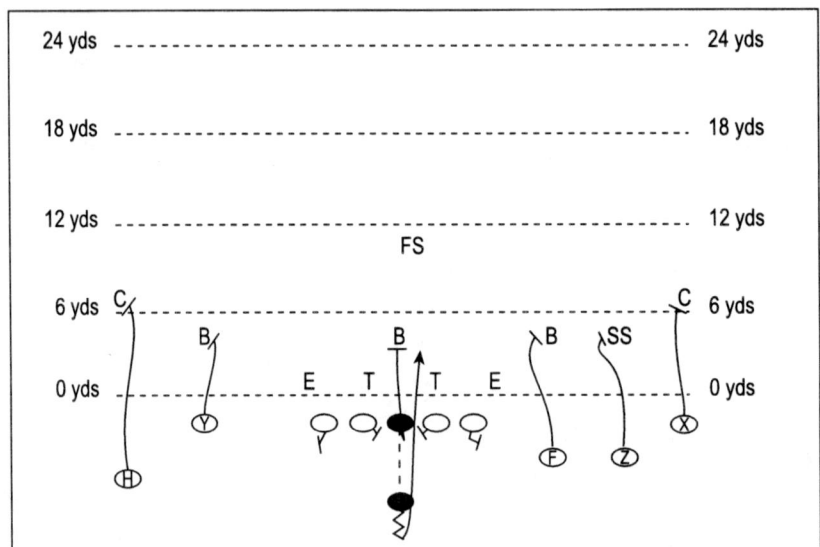

Diagram 8-6. Quarterback draw

Toss Reverse

The toss reverse is an excellent misdirection play off of a basic offensive run play. Many combinations are possible: reverse, fake reverse, halfback pass, and throwback to quarterback. This play is a great option on run-down situations, especially after the running game has been established.

Assignments:

Quarterback: Reverse out—execute the toss; drop the hands, making sure that backside pursuit knows that you do not have the ball; after the reverse exchange, become a blocker.

Flanker (Z): Jab step and execute a reverse; gain ground on the reverse track.

Split end (X): Push upfield and crack the near safety.

Tight end (Y): Block toss run play (aggressive).

Fullback (F): Block toss run play (force).

Halfback (H): Counter step—secure toss; run four to five hard strides for flow; handoff exchange with the reverse man (Z).

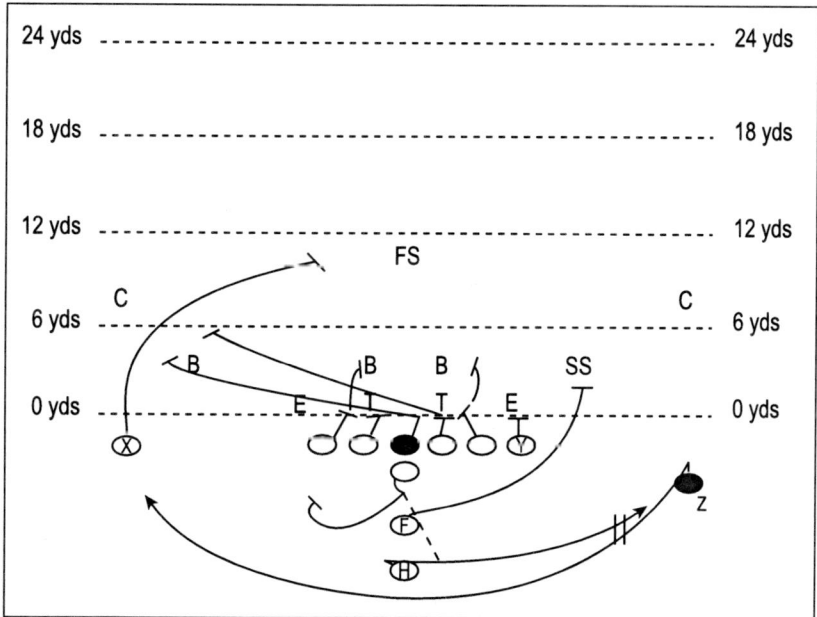

Diagram 8-7. Toss Reverse

Zone Reverse

The zone reverse is an excellent misdirection play off of a basic single-back running play (inside zone). It is great versus defenses that flow quickly to the ball. The offensive line should initially make blocks for zone left; the right tackle has a key arc block to bust loose the reverse man.

Assignments:

Quarterback: Open-fake zone run; pitch the ball to the reverse man (Z).

Flanker (Z): Jab step and execute a reverse; gain ground on the reverse track.

Split end (X): Push upfield and block the near safety.

Tight end (Y): Secure the end man on the line of scrimmage—be aggressive; do not allow upfield penetration.

Third wide receiver (F): Push upfield and crack the near safety.

Halfback (H): Execute a great zone run fake.

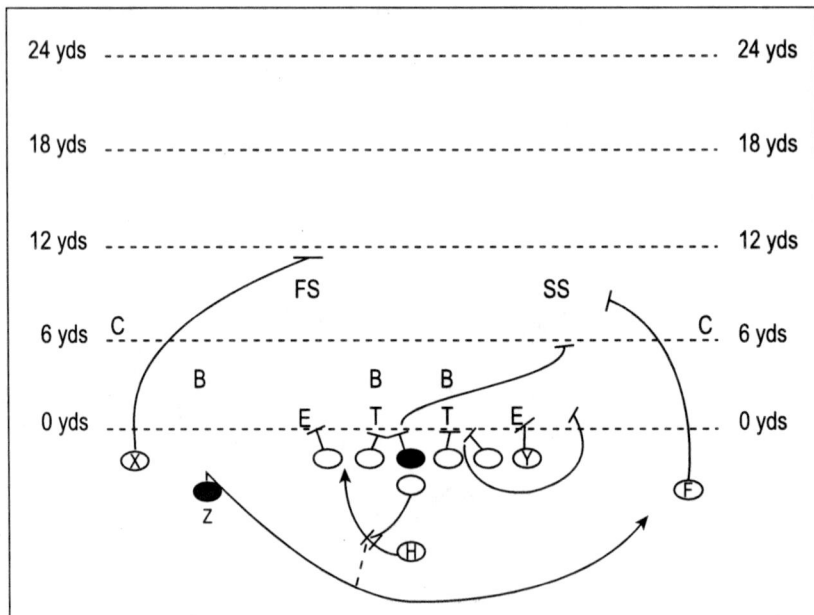

Diagram 8-8. Zone reverse

Lead Flea Flicker

The lead flea flicker is a special play versus a very aggressive defense, especially aggressive defensive backs. It is very important to choose the proper situation (down/distance and field location) in which to win the play.

Assignments:

Quarterback: Reverse out; hand-off the ball deep to the halfback; set up seven to nine yards deep to receive the pitch; read flanker to split end.

Flanker (Z): Execute stalk block—then release on a takeoff route; be patient.

Split end (X): Execute stalk block—then release on a post route; be patient.

Tight end (Y): Block aggressively for play-action pass.

Fullback (F): Sell the lead block for play-action pass—do not block downfield.

Halfback (H): Secure handoff on lead play; attack the line of scrimmage under control; pitch the ball back to quarterback.

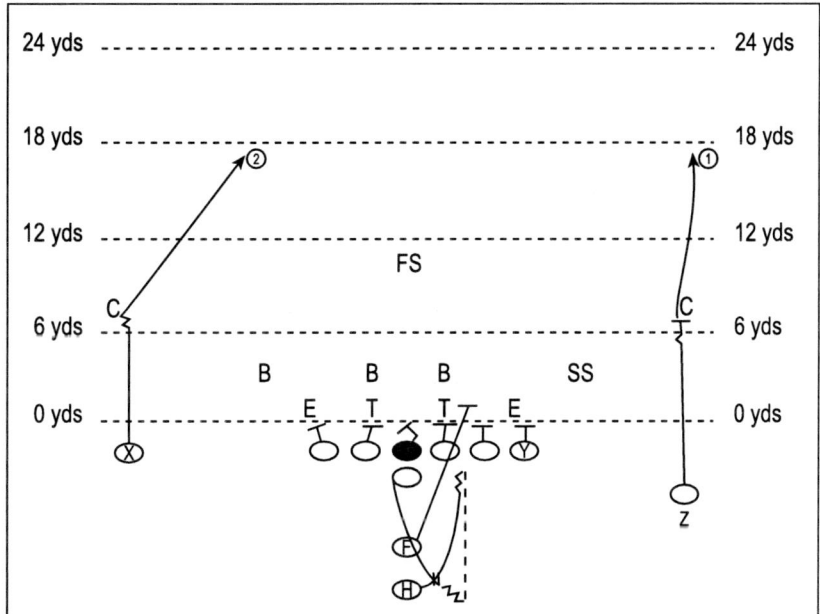

Diagram 8-9. Lead flea flicker

Zone Naked Throwback

The zone naked throwback is a special play-action pass with big-play potential. If offers an excellent opportunity to utilize a gifted running back's pass-catching ability. It is most effective when called in situations where a running play is anticipated.

Assignments:

Quarterback: Open—execute zone fake; carry out the naked play-action; read the split end on a post route and the halfback on a wheel route.

Flanker (Z): Release outside on a takeoff route.

Split end (X): Run a post route; align with a six-to-eight yard split.

Tight end (Y): Block play-action pass protection.

Third wide receiver or fullback (F): Run a pivot route; be prepared for a possible hot throw versus pressure.

Halfback (H): Fake zone run; execute a wheel route (stay wide); versus blitz coverage; look quickly for the ball.

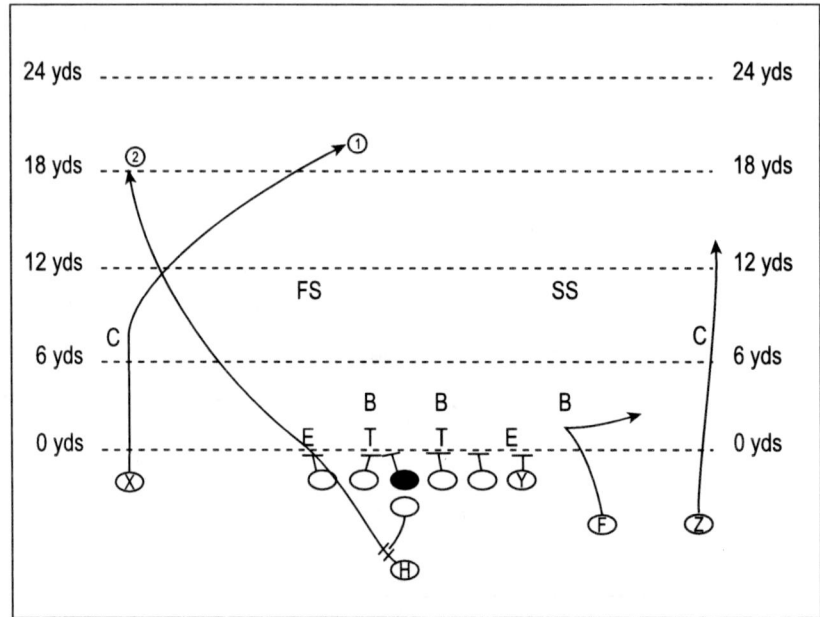

Diagram 8-10. Zone naked throwback

Zone Reverse Pass

The zone reverse pass is a great opportunity to get the ball into a playmaker's hands. This play is designed to complement basic reverse runs and is an excellent choice to will jump-start an offense early in a game.

Assignments:

Quarterback: Open—fake zone run; pitch the ball to the flanker on a reverse.

Flanker (Z): Jab step; secure pitch, and execute the reverse. Pass reads: flanker on crack corner route; split end on crossing route; run.

Split end (X): Run a crossing route at a depth of eight to 10 yards.

Tight end (Y): Block reverse pass play-action protection; do not allow penetration.

Third wide receiver (F): Run a crack corner route; be patient.

Halfback (H): Fake a zone run.

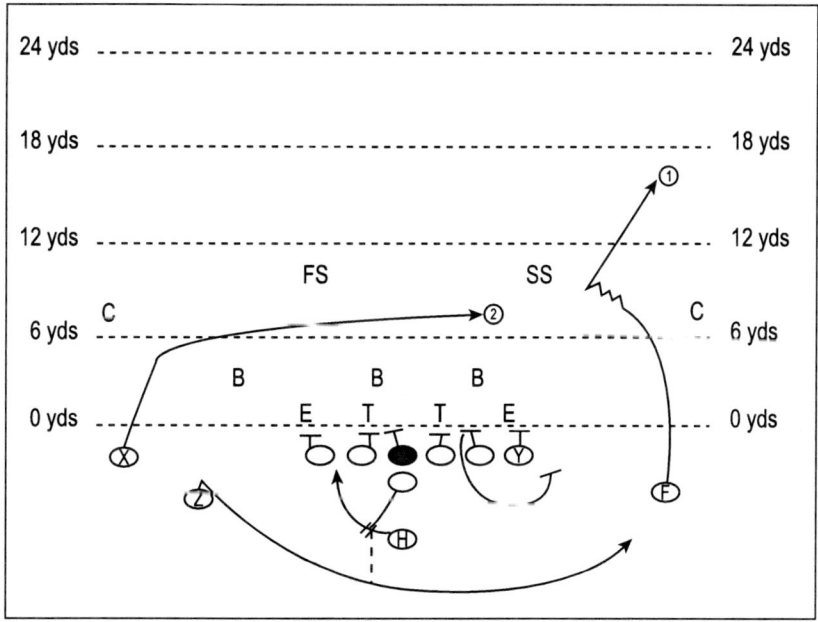

Diagram 8-11. Zone reverse pass

Zone Dummy Pass

The zone dummy pass is a special pass play that is designed to complement a reverse play. It offers a great opportunity to utilize a running back as a downfield pass receiver and can be an excellent play to execute in situations where a new play is anticipated.

Assignments:

Quarterback: Open—fake the zone run; fake the reverse to the flanker, and then drift outside. Pass reads: post; halfback on wheel.

Flanker (Z): Fake reverse (don't look back).

Split end (X): Run a post route.

Tight end (Y): Secure the backside of play-action protection.

Third wide receiver (F): Release on a six to eight yard crossing route.

Halfback (H): Execute a sloppy zone run fake and then release on a wheel route (stay wide).

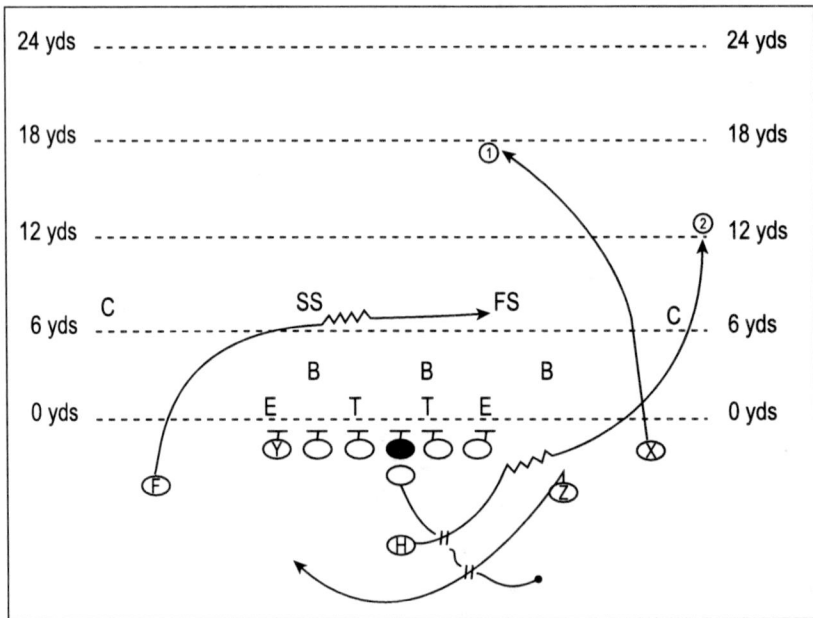

Diagram 8-12. Zone Dummy Pass

Jailbreak Wide Receiver Special

The jailbreak wide receiver special is designed to complement a jailbreak wide receiver screen. It can be a great play to win against a defense that aggressively attacks the screen to stop it before it develops.

Assignments:

Quarterback: Gun alignment—pump-fake the split end on a jailbreak screen, and then drift back. The halfback is his first read (this has big-play potential).

Flanker (Z): Release outside on a takeoff route.

Split end (X): Sell the fake of the jailbreak screen route; throw the hands up to simulate a response to a ball in flight.

Tight end (Y): Block solid pass protection.

Third wide receiver (F): Run a seam route (down the hash).

Halfback (H): Sell the fake kick-out block for the jailbreak screen, and then release on a wheel route (stay wide) as the primary receiver; look quickly for the ball versus a blitz.

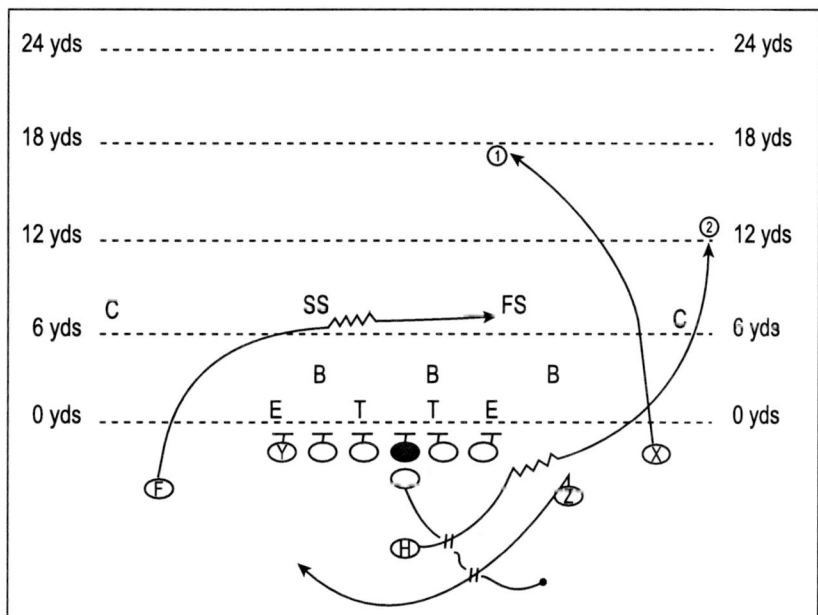

Diagram 8-13. Jailbreak wide receiver special

Sprint Rub

The sprint rub is an excellent pass play versus man or blitz coverages. The offense can use multiple formations/motions to help disguise the play. It is great in short-yardage and goal-line situations and is a high percentage play. The offensive line and back will execute sprint protection.

Assignments:

Quarterback: Sprint out—be prepared to throw on the fifth step; against man coverage, hit the fullback; against zone coverage, read fullback/flanker/split end.

Flanker (Z): Against man coverage, execute a rub route for the fullback; against zone coverage, pivot outside at a depth of four to six yards.

Split end (X): Release outside on a takeoff route.

Tight end (Y): Execute backside of sprint-out protection (hinge).

Third wide receiver or back (F): Run a short route—gaining depth to three to four yards.

Halfback (H): Execute sprint-out protection.

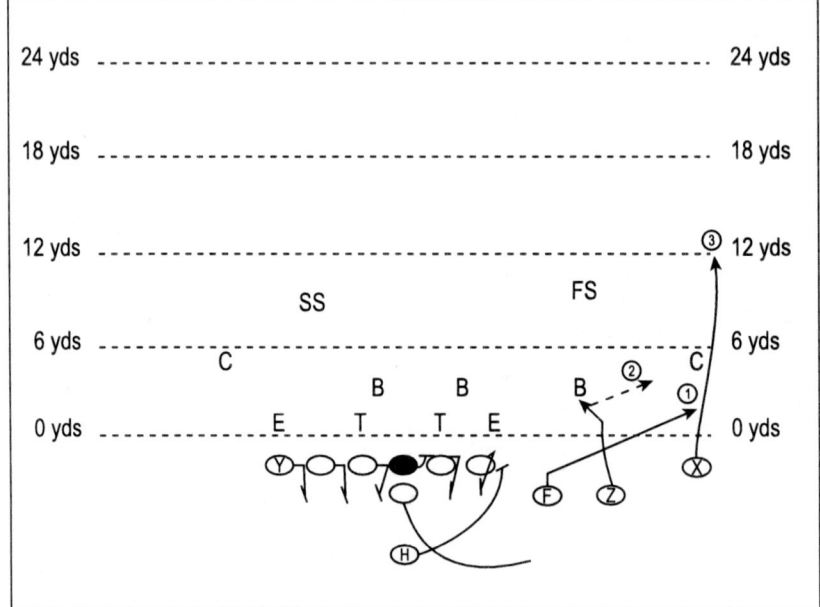

Diagram 8-14. Sprint rub

Sprint Bomb

The sprint bomb is a great pass play versus a defensive coverage that rotates quickly when reacting to sprint action. The quarterback must have a strong arm to execute this play properly. The offensive line and back will execute sprint protection.

Assignments:

Quarterback: Gun alignment—secure the snap; sprint five to seven yards and set the feet for a big-league throw.

Flanker (Z): Run a six to eight yard sail route; if a breakdown in protection occurs, look for the ball (safety valve).

Split end (X): Release outside on a takeoff route.

Fourth wide receiver (Y): Run a deep post route and then break back on a deep corner route.

Third wide receiver or back (F): Seal the edge for a sprint protection; look for a linebacker scraping.

Halfback (H): Execute sprint protection.

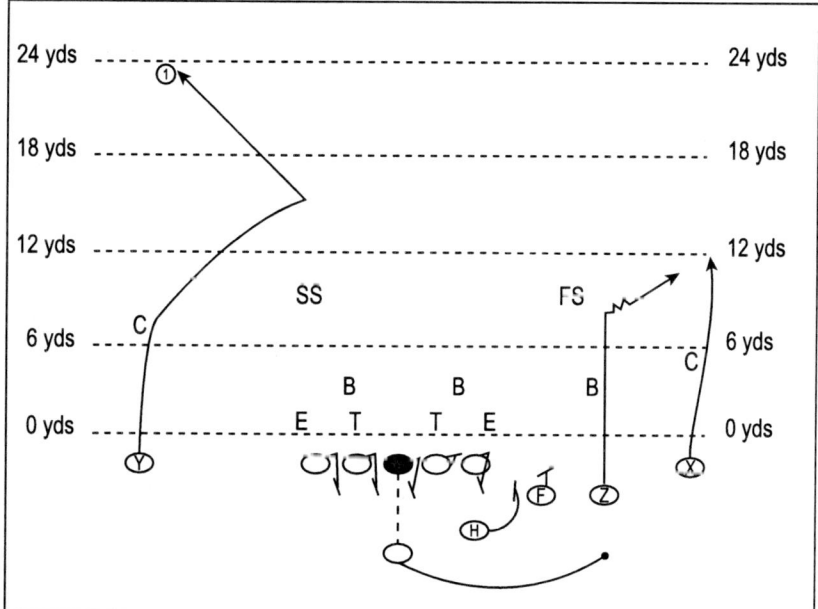

Diagram 8-15. Sprint bomb

Jailbreak Wide Receiver Screen (Type I)

This play is an effective screen that is designed to combat an aggressive pass rush and create an opportunity to put the ball into a playmaker's hands. An offensive player who returns punts would be great choice as the key player for this play because he will more than likely have the patience and skills to use his blockers properly. The type I play has a wide receiver executing the key kick-out block. The offensive tackles will block five-step pass protection. The center and guards will set the pass/slap defender and release on the proper angle screen side.

Assignments:

Quarterback: Gun alignment—zone coverage; look opposite and then deliver the ball to the screen receiver; against man/blitz coverage, don't look off; rather, find the passing lane for the screen receiver.

Flanker (Z): Jab step, execute the screen, and then catch the pass inside of the offensive tackle's block. After the catch, let the blocks develop (run north/south).

Split end (X): Stalk-block the near defender; against man coverage, run the defender off.

Fourth wide receiver (Y): Stalk-block the near defender; against man coverage, run the defender off.

Third wide receiver (F): Quick release; block the nearest underneath defender aligned on the flanker (screen receiver).

Halfback (H): Swing into position to cut off the backside, underneath defender.

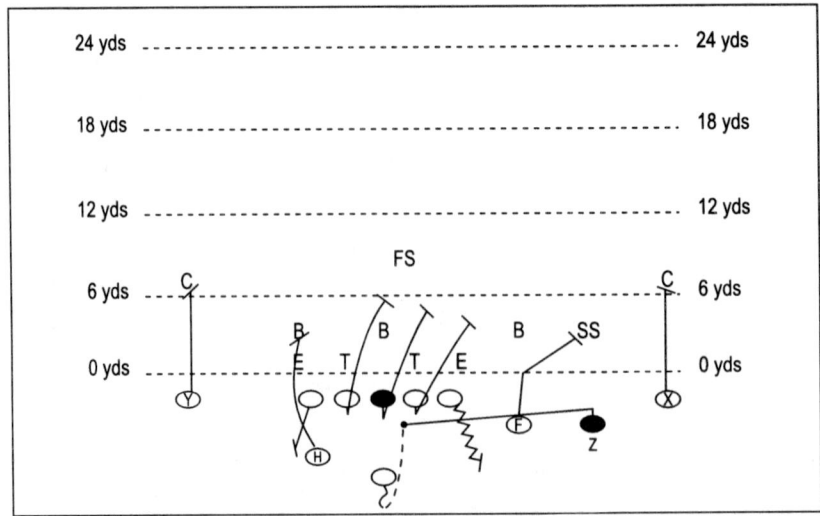

Diagram 8-16. Jailbreak wide receiver screen (type I)

Jailbreak Wide Receiver Screen (Type II)

This play is an effective screen that is designed to combat an aggressive pass rush and create an opportunity to put the ball into a playmaker's hands. An offensive player that returns punts would excel with this play because he will have the patience to use his blockers properly. The type II play has a back executing the key kick-out block. The offensive tackles will block five-step pass protection. The center and guards will set the pass/slap defender and release on the proper angle screen side.

Assignments:

Quarterback: Gun alignment—zone coverage; look opposite, and then deliver the ball to the screen receiver; against man/blitz coverage, don't look off; rather find the passing lane for the screen receiver.

Flanker (Z): Stalk-block the near defender; against man coverage, run the defender off.

Split end (X): Jab step and execute a screen; catch the pass inside of the offensive tackle's block.; after the catch, let the blocks develop (run north/south).

Tight end (Y): Release and get into position to cut off the underneath defender.

Third wide receiver (F): Release and block the near deep safety.

Halfback (H): Quick release; block the nearest underneath defender aligned on the split end (screen receiver).

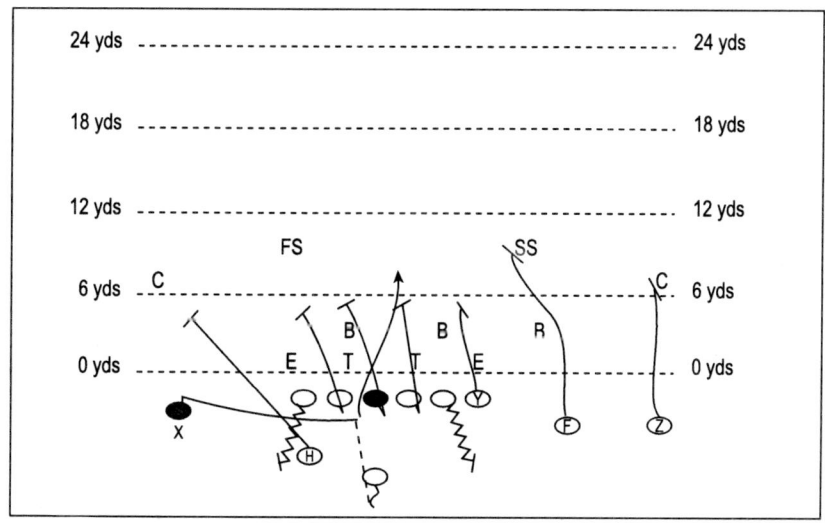

Diagram 8-17. Jailbreak wide receiver screen (type II)

Reach Quick Screen

The reach quick screen is a play that is designed to complement a sprint-out passing game. It is very effective versus a defense that rotates quickly to sprint action. When executing this play, it is beneficial to send the flanker in motion because it will be difficult to press him.

Assignments:

Quarterback: Execute the sprint out (full flow)—gain depth, set the feet, and deliver the ball to the screen receiver; find a passing lane.

Flanker (Z): Zoom motion five to seven yards outside of the weak offensive tackle; jab step—catch the ball behind the line of scrimmage.

Split end (X): Execute a deep stalk-block (search for the far safety).

Tight end (Y): Execute sprint protection.

Fullback (F): Execute sprint protection.

Halfback (H): Execute sprint protection.

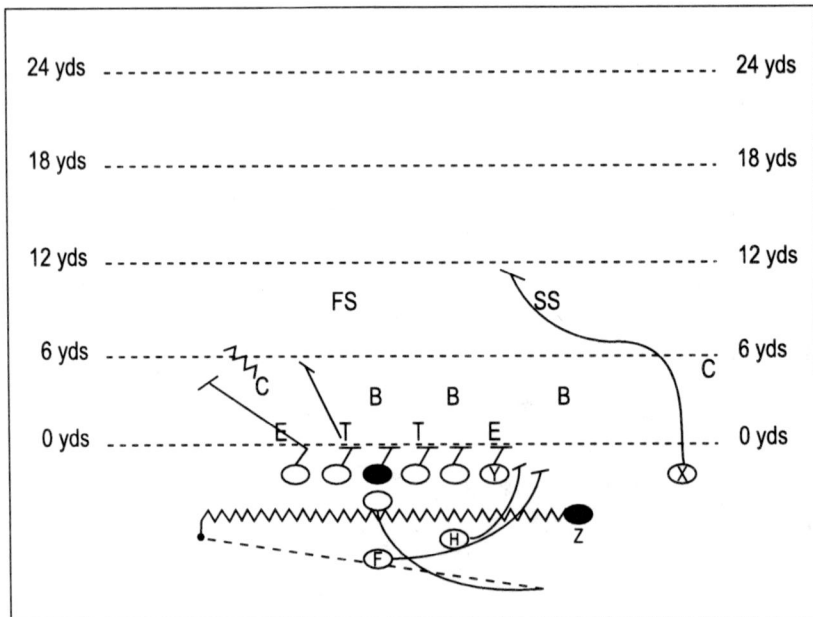

Diagram 8-18. Reach quick screen

Dummy Reverse Quarterback Screen

The dummy reverse quarterback screen is a special play that is designed to complement the reverse package. This play also allows the quarterback to be involved as a pass receiver. As a rule, most defenses will have a difficult time locating a screen to the quarterback.

Assignments:

Quarterback: Open—fake zone run left; pitch the ball to the reverse man (flanker); drift to the screen location; be patient.

Flanker (Z): Execute the reverse; sell the pass downfield, and then deliver the ball to the quarterback.

Split end (X): Push upfield and then crack the near safety.

Tight end (Y): Block the end man on the line of scrimmage; be aggressive.

Third wide receiver (F): Push upfield and then crack the near safety.

Halfback (H): Fake the zone run left; release on a wheel route—block deep outside one-third of field.

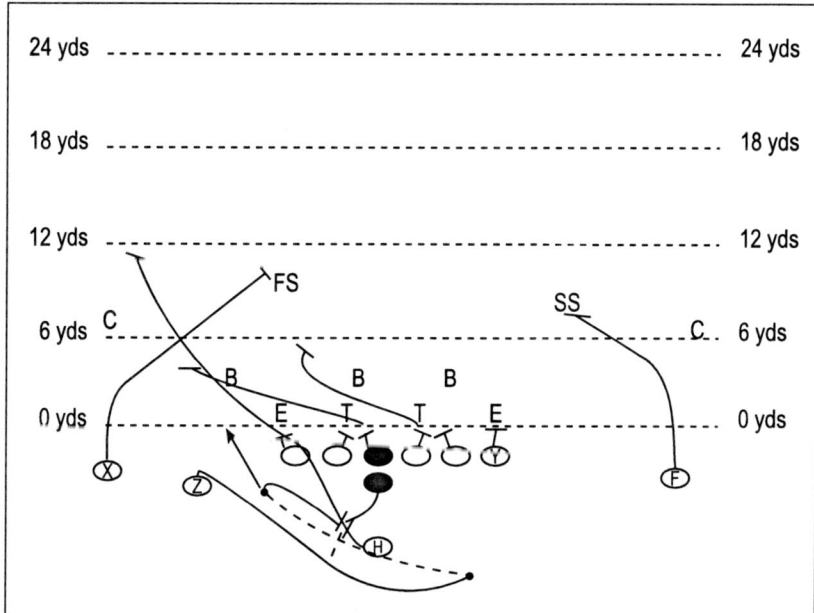

Diagram 8-19. Dummy reverse quarterback screen

Sprint Screen

The sprint screen is an effective play that is designed to complement a sprint-out passing game. This play is very effective versus a defense that rotates quickly on sprint action. The play enables a coach to get the ball to the tight end position. It is particularly effective when employed in the red zone (+30 yard line in).

Assignments:

Quarterback: Execute sprint-out action—gain ground; find a passing lane to deliver the ball to the screen receiver (tight end).

Flanker (Z): Release and block the near deep safety.

Split end (X): Block deep outside one-third of the field.

Tight end (Y): Step inside (hinge) and execute the screen—be patient for two to three seconds; catch the ball behind the line of scrimmage—help find the passing lane.

Third wide receiver (F): Push and crack the near deep safety.

Halfback (H): Execute sprint-out protection.

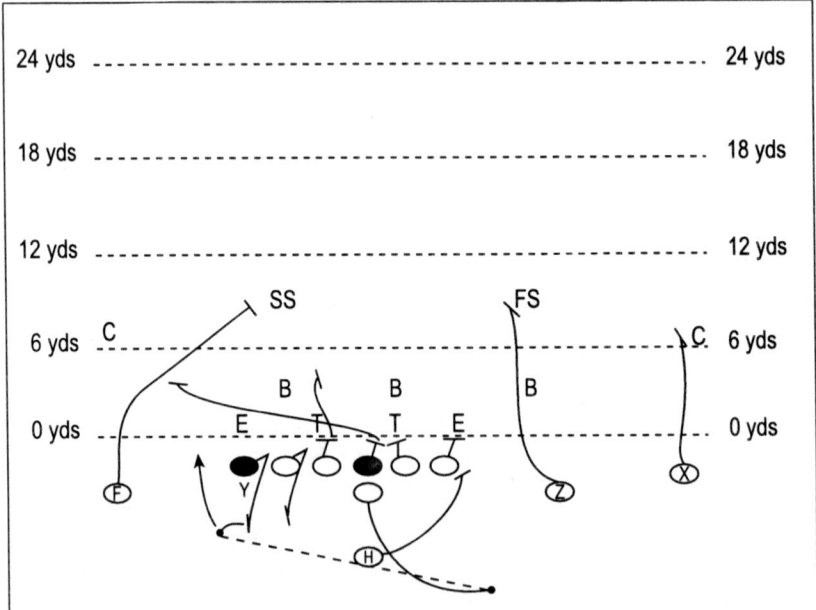

Diagram 8-20. Sprint screen

Middle Screen

The middle screen is an excellent play versus an aggressive pass rush. This play can be executed out of numerous formations. When executing this play, it is important that the quarterback and screen back find a passing lane to deliver the ball.

Assignments:

Quarterback: Gun alignment—sell the pass downfield and then deliver the ball to the screen back.

Flanker (Z): Release and occupy the underneath defender, then block the safety; against man coverage, run off the defender.

Split end (X): Release and block the outside defender; against man coverage, run off the defender.

Fourth wide receiver (Y): Release and occupy the underneath defender, then block the safety; against man coverage, run off the defender.

Third wide receiver (F): Release and block the outside defender; against man coverage, run off the defender.

Halfback (H): Has multiple possible alignments; execute the screen; be patient and let the pass rush develop (hide).

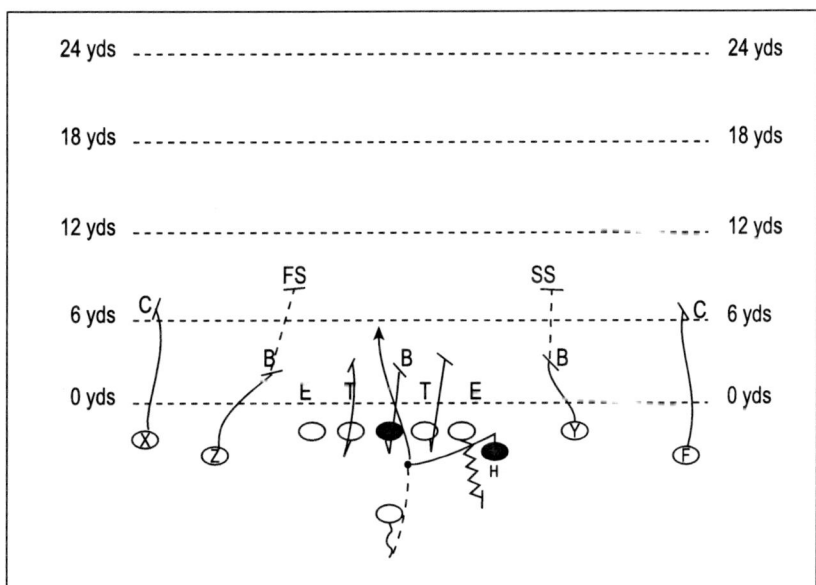

Diagram 8-21. Middle screen

Bench and Up

The bench and up is a pass play with big-play potential that is designed to complement the basic bench/curl pattern. When executed properly, the worst option the quarterback will have on this play is the curl. The bench and up is great play versus aggressive cornerbacks play.

Assignments:

Quarterback: Execute a five-to-seven step drop; read the split end/flanker/halfback.

Flanker (Z): Run a bench-and-up route, selling the bench phase (look back). Motion will help the flanker execute the route with momentum.

Split end (X): Run a 12-yard curl route.

Tight end (Y): Check protection—run an arrow route.

Third wide receiver (F): Run a 12-yard curl route.

Halfback (H): Check protection—run a hook route.

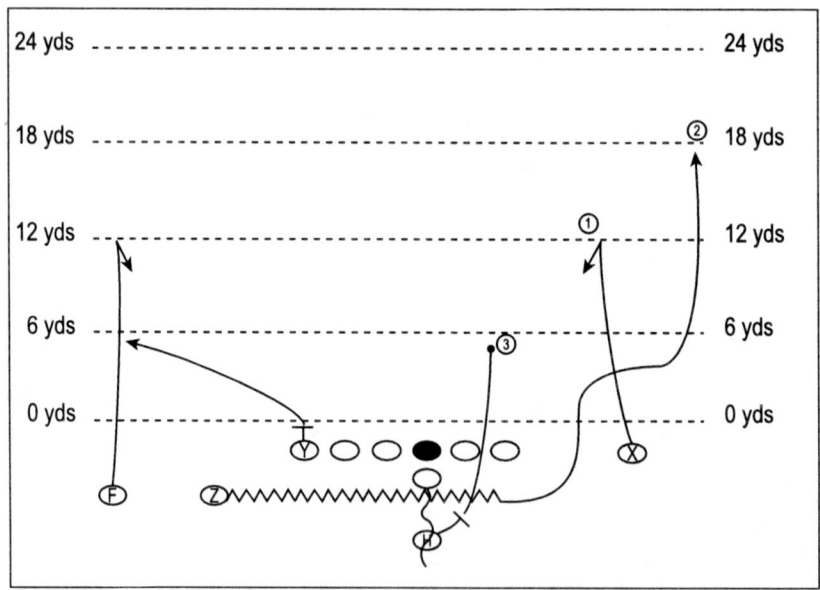

Diagram 8-22. Bench and up

Backs Cross (Fake Draw)

The backs cross (fake draw) play is designed to complement an offense that employs draws. It is a pass play that attacks linebackers in coverage (man or zone). Much of its effectiveness is due to the fact that defenses have a tendency to disregard the back in the passing game after a draw fake.

Assignments:

Quarterback: Gun alignment—fake the draw; against zone coverage, read flanker/tight end or halfback; against man coverage, read the halfback.

Flanker (Z): Run a 12-yard in route; against zone coverage, throttle; against man coverage, accelerate.

Split end (X): Release outside on a takeoff route.

Tight end (Y): Release inside on a cross route; against zone coverage, throttle; against man coverage, accelerate.

Third wide receiver (F): Release outside on a takeoff route.

Halfback (H): Fake the draw; release on a cross route underneath the tight end; against zone coverage, throttle; against man coverage, accelerate. Be prepared for a possible hot throw.

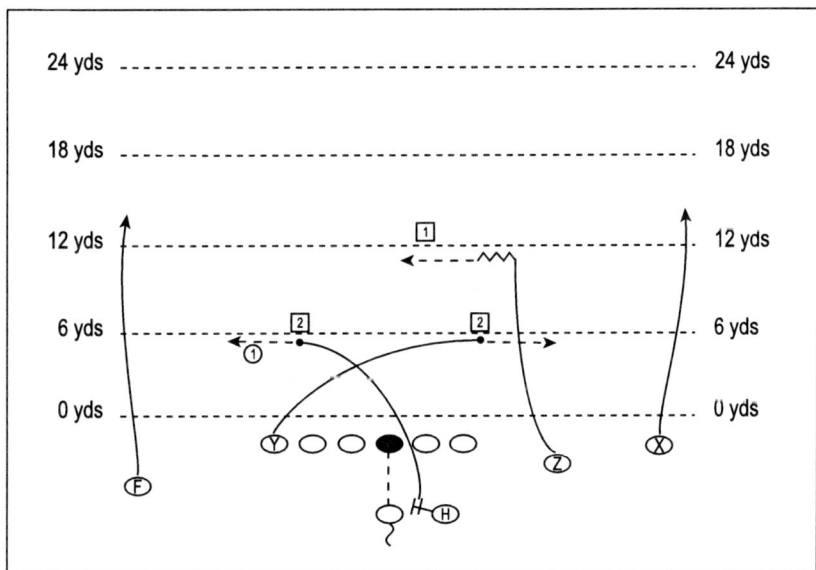

Diagram 8-23. Backs cross (fake draw)

Drags (Flanker Drag)

The drags (flanker drag) is designed to be an effective play versus zone/man/blitz coverages. The drag concept has a natural built-in sight adjustment. The play is flexible to drag any receiver by calling his letter. The next adjacent receiver inside will run the wraparound route.

Assignments:

Quarterback: Executes a five-step drop or gun alignment; against zone coverage, read the third wide receiver wrap around to the flanker drag; against man coverage, read the flanker drag.

Flanker (Z): Execute the drag route (four to six yards deep); against zone coverage, throttle; against man coverage, accelerate.

Split end (X): Release outside on a takeoff route.

Fourth wide receiver (Y): Release outside on a takeoff route; assume a wide split to spread the defense.

Third wide receiver (F): Run a wraparound route (12 yards); against man coverage, accelerate; against zone coverage, throttle. Be alert for man/blitz coverage—rub for drag (flanker).

Halfback (H): Check the protection; release on a swing route on the opposite side of the drag receiver.

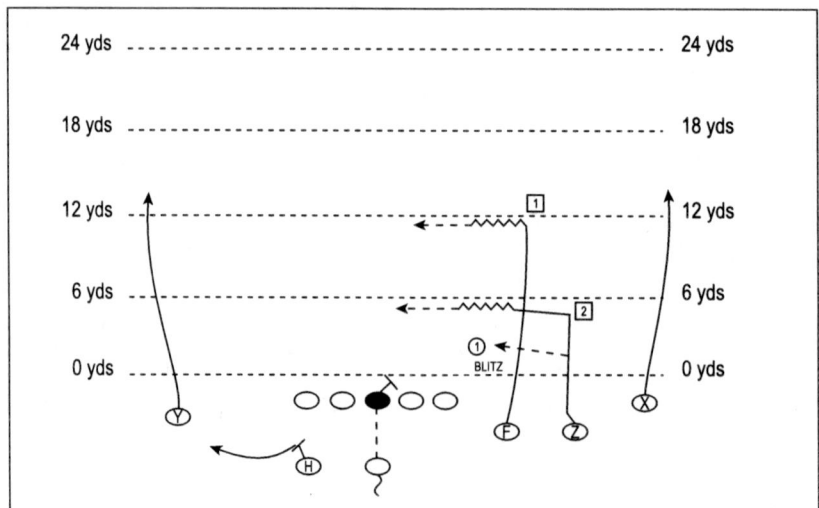

Diagram 8-24. Drags (flanker drag)

Smash (Empty Backfield)

The smash (empty backfield) play has built-in sight adjustments. Prop spacing is very important in order to *stretch* the defense. The quarterback has the following reads:
- Three-deep: read smash/corner (softest side)
- Two-deep: read H/Y/F
- Blitz: read H (who will break away from defender)

Assignments:

Quarterback: Gun alignment—be alert for a blitz.

Flanker (Z): Run a corner route (break at eight yards).

Split end (X): Run a smash route—possible sight adjustment.

Fourth wide receiver (Y): Run a corner route (break at eight yards).

Third wide receiver (F): Run a smash route—possible sight adjustment.

Fifth wide receiver (H): Run a seam route—be alert for a blitz sight adjustment.

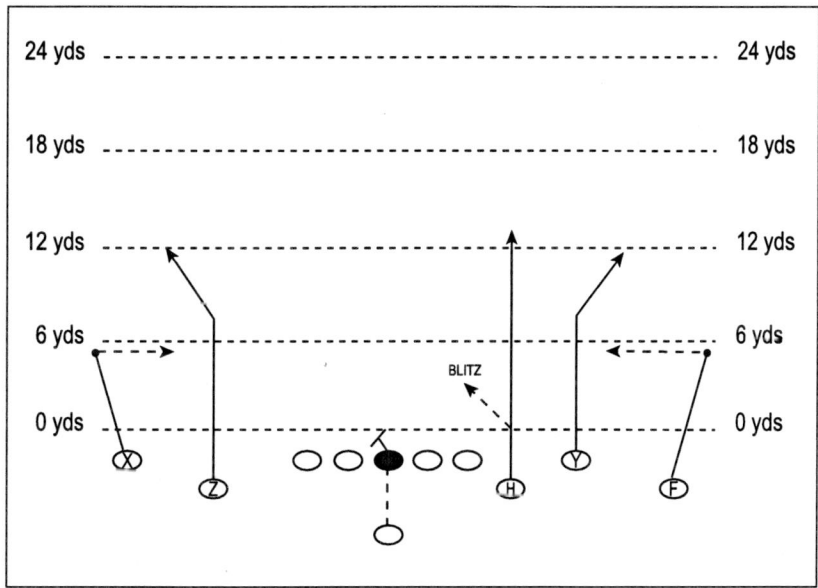

Diagram 8-25. Smash (empty backfield)

Conclusion

Styles and types of football have always run in cycles. Offenses appear to lead the way with new and unique ideas, with the defense having to catch up and defend against the offensive innovations. This forces the offense to move forward again with something new and different to effectively move the football.

Because of the cyclical nature of football, no single best offense exists. The key to success is to settle on a basic concept and then work to become as competent as possible in running that particular style of attack. An important consideration is to recognize that an offense cannot do everything. A coach should establish a primary approach to offense and then augment other phases of his offensive thinking to complement this basic approach. The reason is obvious—practice time! To guild a competent offense, practice time and repetition are necessary. Practice, practice, and more practice should be the standard rule. It is difficult to devote sufficient practice time to becoming skilled at all of the various offensive philosophies available.

Remember, football is a game of execution. The teams that execute the best are the teams that usually win. Teams that execute well rarely beat themselves, so they are defeated only when another team is superior in manpower and physical skills. To execute properly, players should practice and become proficient at their individual skills. Individuals then must blend those skills into a team effort, with everyone working as hard as possible for the team.

About the Author

Charlie Stubbs is in his third season on the University of Tulsa coaching staff and serves as offensive coordinator and quarterbacks' coach. He has 17 years of experience as a collegiate assistant coach, including 10 seasons as an offensive coordinator and three years as passing game coordinator.

In his first season at Tulsa, the Hurricane offense ranked 23rd nationally in rushing offense, an improvement of 63 places from the previous year; 28th in scoring offense, a jump of 73 spots from 2002; and 51st in total offense, an improvement of 54 spots from the previous season. Tulsa averaged 387.8 yards in total offense, 191.7 rushing yards, and 30.8 points per game in 2003.

In his previous position, Stubbs spent three seasons (1998–2000) as passing game coordinator and quarterbacks' coach at Alabama. He helped Alabama make appearances in the 1998 Music City Bowl and the Orange Bowl following the 1999 season. The Crimson Tide was also crowned SEC Champions in 1999. Stubbs was named the 1999 SEC Offensive Coordinator of the Year.

Prior to his stint at Alabama, Stubbs served as the offensive coordinator of four different universities: UNLV (1996–1997), where he also coached the quarterbacks; Tennessee-Martin (1995), where he also coached the quarterbacks and wide receivers; Memphis (1994); and Oregon State (1987–1990).

His UNLV teams ranked second in the Western Athletic Conference and ninth nationally in passing offense in 1996, while leading the WAC in 1997 and finishing that season ranked 12th in NCAA statistics. His Tennessee-Martin offense in 1995 ranked first in the league in passing offense and fifth nationally in NCAA Division I-AA.

At Oregon State, Stubbs began as receivers' and tight ends' coach for the 1985 and 1986 seasons, before being promoted to offensive coordinator in 1987. His offenses were ranked among the PAC-10's top three each season in passing offense, and ranked 10th nationally in 1987 and sixth in 1988.

He began his collegiate coaching career as a graduate assistant on LaVell Edwards' staff at BYU in 1983, and in 1984 was a member of the BYU coaching staff that led the Cougars to the national championship. Before that, he was a high school coach at three different schools in South Carolina.

In his career, Stubbs has coached seven all-conference quarterbacks, and had three quarterbacks earn All-American honors: Oregon State's Erik Wilhelm, and freshman All-Americans Jon Denton of UNLV and Tyler Watts of Alabama. He also coached Andrew Zow, the all-time leading passer at the University of Alabama.

Stubbs began his collegiate playing career at Wofford College, but after suffering an injury, transferred to BYU. He earned his bachelor's degree in 1978 and his master's degree in physical education in 1984, both from BYU.

Stubbs and his wife, Sandra, both originally from Charleston, South Carolina, have four children: Troy, Jay, Kim, and Kyle.